Conflicts and Crises in the Composition Classroom

Also in the CrossCurrents series

Attending to the Margins
Writing, Researching, and Teaching on the Front Lines

Coming of Age
The Advanced Writing Curriculum

Coming to Class
Pedagogy and the Social Class of Teachers

Composition, Pedagogy, and the Scholarship of Teaching

The Dissertation and the Discipline
Reinventing Composition Studies

Feminist Empirical Research
Emerging Perspectives on Qualitative and Teacher Research

Foregrounding Ethical Awareness in Composition and English Studies

Getting Restless
Rethinking Revision in Writing Instruction

Good Intentions
Writing Center Work for Postmodern Times

Grading in the Post-Process Classroom
From Theory to Practice

Gypsy Academics and Mother-Teachers
Gender, Contingent Labor, and Writing Instruction

Kitchen Cooks, Plate Twirlers, and Troubadours
Writing Program Administrators Tell Their Stories

Know and Tell
A Writing Pedagogy of Disclosure, Genre, and Membership

Life-Affirming Acts

Miss Grundy Doesn't Teach Here Anymore
Popular Culture and the Composition Classroom

The Mythology of Voice

Outbursts in Academe
Multiculturalism and Other Sources of Conflict

The Politics of Writing Centers

The Politics of Writing in the Two-Year College

Race, Rhetoric, and Composition

Resituating Writing
Constructing and Administering Writing Programs

A Rhetoric of Pleasure
Prose Style and Today's Composition Classroom

Textual Orientations
Lesbian and Gay Students and the Making of Discourse Communities

Writing in an Alien World
Basic Writing and the Struggle for Equality in Higher Education

Conflicts and Crises in the Composition Classroom

—and What Instructors Can Do About Them

EDITED BY
Dawn Skorczewski and Matthew Parfitt

New Perspectives in Rhetoric and Composition
CHARLES I. SCHUSTER, SERIES EDITOR

Boynton/Cook Publishers
HEINEMANN
Portsmouth, NH

Boynton/Cook Publishers, Inc.
A subsidiary of Reed Elsevier Inc.
361 Hanover Street
Portsmouth, NH 03801–3912
www.boyntoncook.com

Offices and agents throughout the world

Library of Congress Cataloging-in-Publication Data
Conflicts and crises in the composition classroom—and what instructors can do about them / edited by Dawn Skorczewski and Matthew Parfitt.
    p. cm. — (CrossCurrents)
    Includes bibliographical references.
    ISBN 0-86709-541-5 (acid-free paper)
    1. English language—Rhetoric—Study and teaching.   2. Report writing—Study and teaching (Higher).   3. Conflict management.   4. Crisis management.   I. Skorczewski, Dawn.
II. Parfitt, Matthew.   III. CrossCurrents (Portsmouth, N.H.)

PE1404. C6336 2003
808'.042'0711—dc21   2002153414

Editor: Charles I. Schuster
Production service: TechBooks
Production coordinator: Elizabeth Valway
Cover design: Suzanne Heiser
Manufacturing: Steve Bernier

Printed in the United States of America on acid-free paper
07 06 05 04 03   DA 1 2 3 4 5

For Barrie Stevens

Contents

Introduction
Dawn Skorczewski and Matthew Parfitt   ix

PART I THE USES OF RESISTANCE

1 **The Chattering of Timothy Strossmeyer, or
   Discipline and the Oppressed**
   Christine Jespersen, Western State College   1

2 **The Angry Student with the C+**
   Ann Dean, University of Southern Maine   7

3 **Wielding Authority in a Nonauthoritarian Classroom**
   Victoria Arthur, Washington State University   13

4 **The Unwelcome Rhetor in Our Midst**
   Brad Peters, Northern Illinois University   20

5 **When Underlife Takes Over**
   An Insight on Student Resistance and Classroom Dynamics
   Suzanne Diamond, Youngstown State University   27

6 **"Is It My Problem if They Can't Keep up with Me?"**
   *Ball Hogs, Point Guards, and Student Participation
   in the Composition Classroom*
   John Regan, Boston University   34

PART II RACE, CLASS, AND THE LANGUAGE OF SCHOOLING

7 **White Indian Up Front**
   *Building Learning Communities in the
   "Postcolonial"/Indigenized Classroom*
   Paul W. DePasquale, University of Winnipeg   41

8 **Detecting the Camouflaged Conflicts**
   *Blackness, Whiteness, and Language
   Difference in Basic Writing Courses*
   Priscilla Perkins, Roosevelt University   51

9   **"What's the Point?"**
    Stephen Dilks, University of Missouri, Kansas City   56

10 **Pedagogy and Apocalypse**
    How to Have a Productive Discussion in the Context of a Race Riot
    T. R. Johnson, University of New Orleans   64

11 **Race in Class**
    Students, Teaching, and Stories
    Linda Adler-Kassner, Eastern Michigan University   69

12 **The One Who Got Away**
    Reflections on a Teacher's Remorse
    Deborah Gussman, The Richard Stockton College of New Jersey   81

PART III COURSE DESIGN AND ASSIGNMENTS

13 **"Some People Just Don't Write Well"**
    Composing and Grading Amid Conflict in the Classroom
    Susanmarie Harrington, Indiana University
    Purdue University Indianapolis   88

14 **How Not to Lead a Class Discussion**
    Dawn Skorczewski, Emerson College   97

15 **Teaching Without Armor**
    Eric V. Martin, Governors State University   104

16 **Plagiarism Might Go Away if We Don't Talk about It**
    Jon Olson, The Pennsylvania State University   109

17 **Room for "Us" to Play**
    The Teacher as Midwife
    Matthew Parfitt, Boston University   113

    Afterword
    Difficulty for Whom?: Teachers' Discourse About Difficult Students
    Hugh English, Queen's College-CUNY   119

    Contributors   125

Introduction

Homines dum docent discunt. (Men learn even while they teach).
—Seneca (4 BCE–65 AD), *Letters* 7.8.

About halfway through Dawn's graduate course in The Teaching of Composition, a student asked, "Why is it that you don't tell us more stories about your struggles in the classroom? This is how we really learn about what it means to teach writing." Several other students chimed in their agreement. For a moment, silence settled on the room. Dawn found it hard to say why anecdotes about her teaching had not been more present in this classroom. Perhaps it was because discussing her experiences as a teacher might make her appear egotistical. But it seemed also to reflect a natural desire for self-protection: What would students think of their instructor, the Director of Composition, if they saw her failures exposed in a class designed to teach them how to teach?

In effect, these graduate students were articulating a theory of learning how to teach that is grounded in a notion of difficulty. Their question suggested that "difficulty" does not represent some failure on the part of the instructor to perform adequately, but emerges instead as a necessary by-product of the composition instructor's close involvement with student learning. The writers in this collection share the conviction that stories about a teacher's moments of crisis in the classroom afford invaluable sources of knowledge about our craft. It's the difficult moments that often resonate most deeply with us (sometimes even cause us to obsess), and to seek out close colleagues for advice or reassurance. And when we are willing to show ourselves to be flawed, evolving, and still struggling to learn, we enter into some of the most exciting and powerful conversations about classroom practice that we can have—conversations that really make a difference in what we do. The premise of this book is that the subject matter of these rewarding conversations reveals our pedagogical assumptions and convictions, and enables us to reexamine them.

This collection invites readers to explore several aspects of a teacher's difficulty in the classroom: how it emerges, what we are experiencing and observing as it occurs, and what we learn from these encounters with it. It offers true stories from writing teachers who have turned crises into occasions for revisiting their most deeply held pedagogical convictions and assumptions. Robert Coles (1990) argues that we might best look for our theories in stories, rather than seeking stories to suit existing theoretical tenets. This book seeks to capitalize on this "thick" quality of narrative. *Stories,* we would suggest, are the threads that connect the concrete experience of classroom practice to the abstract generalization of theory, but they are threads that can be twisted and turned in any number of directions. The essays in this book may tease insights and lessons out of their narratives, but such lessons remain grounded in narrative and therefore closer to practice. Thus, these stories might be read as the starting points for reflection and discussion, rather than end points. The writers invite us to look closely at critical moments, to think with them about how to address the difficulty they present, and to consider how we can improve our teaching by attending to the fears and doubts that lie just beneath the surfaces of our classrooms.

It is often tempting to suppose that problems in the classrooms reflect the instructor's inexperience, laziness, or poor judgment, or the students' inexperience, laziness, and poor judgment. When we do this, we approach difficult situations in the classroom from competing directions: the teacher's or the student's. Rarely do we consider the students and teachers together as a unit—a group of people making meaning together. Yet when we do think about classrooms this way, we begin to investigate some of our oldest pedagogical wisdom from an entirely different perspective: not what "they" might have done, or what "you" or "I" might have done, but what *we,* together and separately, bring to each encounter in the classroom.

The situations discussed in these essays are familiar to many readers: they concern students who insist on doing an assignment other than the one required; students who persistently dominate discussions; students who react violently against their peers in a workshop; and students who divide against each other along racial, ethnic, or gender lines. Although we are intimately connected to such situations as writing teachers, we know from experience that there are no simple solutions to such problems. The fact that we share similar challenges as teachers but cannot solve our problems quickly and simply lies at the center of this book. Dynamic systems theorists R. C. Schank and J. B. Cleave write: "Nearly everyone would agree that experience is the best teacher. What many fail to realize is that experience is the *only* teacher" (1995, p. 181). The essayists in this collection presume that much of what we might call "the problem" can only be understood through an examination of the details and nuances of a particular classroom: the interactions between a unique group of students and a particular teacher.

This is fundamentally a book about revision. As compositionists, we draw from theories of reading and writing that emphasize the value of teaching students to explore difficulty in their own and others' texts. In "Revision Strategies of Student Writers and Experienced Adult Writers," Nancy Sommers (1980) explains that experienced writers actively seek out dissonance as they revise their essays; they begin to reshape what they write from that vantage point. When working with student writers, we intervene in the surface appearance of smoothness and steer them toward whatever problematizes their arguments, so that they can begin a revision that brings greater depth and complexity to their work. This book is about the need to be equally suspicious of easefulness in the classroom, the need to focus attention on the moments of difficulty in order to make maximal use of them. It is precisely the painful moments of dissonance that are worthy of reflection and that ultimately reveal new perspectives and new practices. Freireian (Freire, 1970) "problem-posing" pedagogues who offer students positions of authority in the classroom should also, it seems, take their own problems as teachers seriously—and for the same reason: teachers must model what it means to learn, to confront real-world problems as the source of genuine learning, and remain skeptical of the conventional wisdom.

This book is divided into four parts. The first, "The Uses of Resistance," contains essays in which writers explore the lessons learned from some of their most awkward and vexatious interactions with students. As the title implies, however, student resistance may become the catalyst for a reexamination of pedagogy. Part II, "Race, Class, and the Language of Schooling," explores the conflicts that arise from the diversities of culture, race, language, and experience in our classrooms. Part III, "Course Design and Assignments," explores how the syllabus, assignments, grading, and goals of a composition course can both shape and be shaped by moments of difficulty in the classroom. In the afterword, Hugh English examines the very discourse of "difficulty" in the classroom. Difficulty, he suggests, might be seen as an opportunity to reexamine the ways that the instructor allows the classroom to become a world created in his or her own image, and to consider ways that instructors might be able to revise that world.

If composition is "a teaching subject," as Joseph Harris (1996) calls it, a discipline to which the business of teaching is central, and if teaching always involves particular teachers and particular students in particular classrooms, then its knowledge can never be entirely reduced to theory or even ideas; it must remain embedded in experience, in stories. And although these stories give rise to reflection, there must always be a remainder that might give rise to further questioning, further doubt, and further reflection. Hence, the essays in this collection, although they do offer tentative solutions and lessons that emerge from their stories of difficult moments, do not necessarily "solve" or dissolve the difficulty they describe. More frequently, the difficulty itself comes to be seen from a fresh perspective, perhaps as an opportunity rather than a problem, perhaps as the sign of an underlying conflict or issue. But as stories, embedded in a particular time and place, concerning unique and complex individuals, they cannot be entirely superceded by their solutions or abstract lessons. Our hope is that these essays will encourage readers to participate in the process of reflection and to continue it in light of their own experience.

Writing is fundamental to learning and knowing, and it occupies a central position in a liberal education. It is the site where the self meets the world, and consequently, the writing course is a risky, high-stakes enterprise, perhaps the course that more than any other, courts disaster. Because no two teachers, no two classrooms, no two students are exactly alike, because we must be "learning as we teach," the teaching of composition remains endlessly fascinating and endlessly challenging.

Works Cited

Coles, Robert. 1990. *The Call of Stories: Teaching and the Moral Imagination.* Boston: Houghton Mifflin.

Freire, Paulo. 1970. *Pedagogy of the Oppressed.* Trans. Myra Bergman Ramos. New York: Seabury P.

Harris, Joseph. 1996. *A Teaching Subject: Composition Since 1966.* Upper Saddle River, NJ: Prentice Hall.

Schank, R. C. and J. B. Cleave. 1995. "Natural Learning, Natural Teaching," in *The Mind, the Brain, and Complex Adaptive Systems,* edited by Harold Morowitz and Jerome L. Singer, 175–202. (Santa Fe Institute Studies in the Sciences of Complexity, Proceedings XXII). Reading, MA: Addison-Wesley.

Sommers, Nancy. 1980. "Revision Strategies of Student Writers and Experienced Adult Writers." CCC, v 31, n 4: 378–388.

Conflicts and Crises in the Composition Classroom

1

The Chattering of Timothy Strossmeyer, or Discipline and the Oppressed

Christine Jespersen

Timothy Strossmeyer. Or "Timothy Stressmaker," as I called him to myself. Not his real appellation, of course, but similar. He sat at the very back left-hand corner of the class. A large man and an even larger presence. Cheerful and good-natured to be sure, but one who could not stop talking, ever. As long as the conversation centered on him, as long as I was calling on him, he was, I suppose, a fair student. Yet whenever another student was speaking or I was speaking, he was talking to the woman who sat directly in front of him or to the two young men who sat to his left. A constant stream of talk about parties and snowboarding and movies. An exhausting talker with no listening skills whatsoever. My usual repertoire of tricks to quiet the talkative had failed miserably, and I was thinking of throwing him out of class.

I admit that I had made several mistakes that had little to do with Timothy Stressmaker. The first was to advertise a first-year general education course entitled "Adventure Literature." My chair was pleased because the course filled past capacity. My course would support the more thinly populated upper-division "The Anglo-Saxon Greats," "T. S. Eliot's Criticism," and "Eighteenth-Century Poetic Humor." I knew a lot about adventure literature and I thought that the subject would be an excellent way to introduce students to the pleasures of literary analysis. What I had not considered was that the recruiting video for our small, mountain college had precious little footage of scholarly types in libraries, of whom we had quite a few, and a lot of footage of snowboarding dudes and dudettes, shred Betties and Bobs (telemark skiers), and class V boaters.

Although the serious types flocked to "Twentieth-Century Poetry," "Representations of Women in the Nineteenth-Century Novel," and "Shakespearean Drama," my course mainly attracted students more interested in outdoor adventures than adventures of the mind. Not that these two interests are mutually exclusive, but in the case of my "Adventure Literature" course, they were nearly so. Although I attempted to make connections between challenges of the body and challenges of the intellect, I made precious few inroads into the 18-year-old snowboarder mind, and I made a note that my next course would be entitled "Grammatical Constructions of the Petrarchan Sonnet."

My next mistake was to make group work the main structure of the course. Not bad in itself, but the room in which I taught was long and narrow. It was packed to capacity and I was stranded at the head of the classroom with Timothy Stressmaker as far away from me as a student could be and still be *in* the classroom. In a related mistake, I set a pattern of allowing students to choose their own groups, so rearranging them met with resistance not only from Stressmaker, but from most of his peers as well.

I also had begun the year with a much too low-key, laid-back approach. My professor persona was exactly wrong for this particular class. Whereas I had hoped to convey that I was open-minded and encouraged various perspectives, instead I seemed to have suggested that absolutely *any* comment was fine regardless of topic. Whereas I had hoped to convey that I was not tediously tied to regulation, instead I seemed to have let it be known that attendance was optional, arrival time was at the students' convenience, and that handing in papers written in crayon, then folded in half was acceptable. In short, whereas I had hoped to convey that I imagined my students as adults with legitimate concerns and ideas, instead I had managed to demonstrate in a very short time that if my students preferred junior high to college, that was perfectly all right with me.

Yet having begun my career at a private school, where a healthy number of students had been discharged from public institutes for disruptive behavior, I was no stranger to discipline problems. I rallied my forces and began to use the techniques I had learned from my year of private school purgatory.

I first tried to garner peer pressure. When Stressmaker opened his mouth inappropriately, I stopped talking and looked at him, all the while breathing deeply and thinking of my summer vacation or the last novel I had read. For most students, this technique works. They realize that they are being disruptive, are embarrassed, and quit talking. Stressmaker, however, went right on chattering. So I went on to Phase Two. I stared. A blank, long stare. The impenetrable kind. The kind that suggests that the student is in deep, deep trouble kind. Meanwhile, I continued to breathe. Predictably, the other students began to tell Stressmaker to be quiet. Eventually, he did quiet down, but the remedy lasted fewer than six minutes and he was back at it again, talking, talking, talking.

The next couple of days continued thus, and I ran through what I found to be a rather more meager repertoire of ideas than I had at first estimated. I took Stressmaker aside and asked him to stop disrupting class. I told him to be quiet in front of his peers. I made him switch seats. All of these remedies gave us temporary relief, but none of them quieted the loquacious Stressmaker for more than a few minutes. He continued with an endless stream of blather, disrupting my concentration, becoming a joke to his classmates.

I decided that I had had enough of Stressmaker, that I had given him a number of chances, and that I was going to ask him to withdraw from the class. My syllabus included a clause, adopted by my department, that allowed me to dismiss disruptive students, and Stressmaker certainly qualified. Yet in spite of the fact that he well-emulated a phonograph with no off switch, I basically liked him. He was beginning to say things in class that genuinely contributed to class discussion. And I did hope that he could be turned into a good student. Of course, I knew that my primary duty was not to Stressmaker, but to the majority of students who deserved to learn something about literary analysis. Yet I decided that another day of Stressmaker would not hurt anyone all that much.

At the same time that I was teaching Adventure Literature, I was preparing to teach a composition course which would feature sections of Paulo Freire's (1970) *Pedagogy of the Oppressed* and Foucault's (1995) *Discipline and Punish*. At first glance, it seemed obvious to me that my mostly white, male students who drove to class in Ford Explorers and recreated with state-of-the-art, titanium mountain bikes had little in common with Freire's "oppressed." Bentham's inmates seemed much closer cousins.

Panopticism, Foucault writes, "is polyvalent in its applications; it serves to reform prisoners, but also . . . to instruct schoolchildren, to confine the insane" (1995, p. 205). "Hmmmm," I mused, "*to instruct schoolchildren, to confine the insane.*" I admit that I dreamed for a while of the "marvelous machine," of catching Stressmaker up in a "power situation of which" he was himself "the bearer," of inducing in him "a state of conscious and permanent visibility," of making my students into "thousands of eyes posted everywhere, mobile attentions ever on the alert,"—in short, of creating the conditions for "the perfection of power" that would "render its actual exercise unnecessary" (Foucault 1995, pp. 201, 202, 214).

What I did not recognize initially was that in spite of my architecturally deficient classroom, I had, in fact, attempted several panoptic disciplinary techniques. With my blank stare, I effectively had became the guard in the central tower who "sees everything without ever being seen" and I had enlisted students as "the instrument of permanent, exhaustive omnipresent surveillance" (Foucault 1995, pp. 202, 214). What I had not induced in Stressmaker was a "permanent state of visibility." He had not become "the principle of his own subjection" (Foucault 1995, p. 202). He had, in no sustained way, internalized disciplinary power.

For Foucault, of course, panopticism is an insidious and dangerous form of power that insinuates itself into the deepest levels of the social body. "It is not," he writes, "that the beautiful totality of the individual is amputated, repressed, altered by our social order, it is rather that the individual is carefully fabricated in it, according to a whole technique of forces and bodies" (1995, p. 217). The stated goals of my first-year literature class involved teaching students to appropriate the methods of literary analysis by entering into dialogue with other students, with me, and with the texts. To some extent, I was training my students in the discipline in Foucault's sense of the word. I was asking them to enter into the discipline of literary studies that involved disciplining the self to use particular methodologies. As I clearly understood from the case of Strossmeyer, the discipline of analysis was not unrelated to the discipline of the body. My most successful students not only appropriated disciplinary ways of seeing and writing, but also disciplined themselves to go to class, do the reading, write the papers, and act appropriately in the classroom. My primary goal, however, was not the "perfection of power." It was, in fact, empowering students with disciplinary methods that I hoped that they would appropriate, see the strengths and limitations of, and eventually go beyond.

One of the tensions in my teaching and in liberatory education, in general, is in teaching students the method of a discipline while allowing them freedom to use the methods and even to overturn them. As tempting as Foucault's "guarantee of order" might have been to me in the Strossmeyer situation, a panoptic classroom was not what I ultimately desired. I knew that a schoolroom in which there was "no copying, no noise, no chatter, no waste of time" by "assuring the ordering of human multiplicities" would also prevent the chaos necessary in the kind of learning that I wanted for my students (Foucault 1995, pp. 201, 218).

I turned, once again, to Friere (1970), who advocates a breaking down of the teacher–student dyad in favor of what he calls "problem-posing" education. "The teacher," Freire writes, " is no longer merely the-one-who-teaches, but one who is himself taught in dialogue with the students, who in turn while being taught also teach" (p. 67). Students and teachers see themselves as part of the world that they are involved in remaking. Freire explains, "Problem posing education affirms men and women as beings in the process of *becoming*— as unfinished, uncompleted beings in and with a likewise unfinished reality" (p. 72).

I had thought quite a lot about Freire's pedagogy in terms of teaching the methodology and content of my discipline in the sense of field of study. I had thought very little about it in terms of discipline in the sense of *behavior*. As I knew, both from Foucault and in a different way from Freire, those two senses of the word were separate only in my mind. In practice, they were always already intertwined. I decided to take what Freire said seriously in the Strossmeyer situation. I needed to stop thinking of my student as an object that needed to be controlled and, instead, think of him as in a process of becoming. I also needed to think of myself as open to being taught.

So I asked Strossmeyer to speak to me after class. I explained that I thought his behavior was making it difficult for the rest of the class to learn. He expressed his dismay. I asked him to come up with a plan for halting his inappropriate conversation—a plan to which I had to agree. He said that he wished to continue sitting in his corner and that he would simply stop talking.

If he talked once when he was supposed to be listening, I could throw him out of class. I protested that I thought he should at least change seats so that the temptation to talk would be less, but he insisted his plan would work and he would take the risk of failure. We shook hands on the deal. Timothy Strossmeyer, I am happy to say, stayed for the duration of the course with few relapses.

Freire argues that because meaningful education takes place in dialogue and because "authentic thinking" cannot be done by the teacher for the student that the "subordination of students to teachers becomes impossible" (1970, p. 64). In the Strossmeyer situation, I did not go as far as Freire probably would have liked in relinquishing my authority. I was fully prepared to throw Strossmeyer out of class. However, I did begin to see Strossmeyer and myself differently. I saw us both as changeable and I saw the classroom as "an unfinished reality" (Freire 1970, p. 72). I also began to envision Strossmeyer as a "re-creator" (Freire 1970, p. 62).

My experience with Strossmeyer made me recognize that the pedagogy that I used in the classroom for teaching my course was at odds with my pedagogy of classroom behavior. In my first year of high school teaching, I had been hired without a teaching certificate and had had no training in classroom "management" or in pedagogy. I survived by talking to more experienced teachers, by attending a workshop on discipline, and by trial and error. I had learned, without knowing it, to take an eclectically Foucaultian approach to discipline.

In graduate school I began to read pedagogical theory as part of my training. My pedagogy—as teaching disciplinary material—was transformed and it was much closer to Freire's philosophies than Foucault's. What I came to understand in working with Strossmeyer was that my methods of dealing with classroom discipline had changed very little. When I thought about making Strossmeyer into a "good" student, I thought about making him into a person who appropriated discipline and knowledge and about a person who behaved appropriately in class. In those early weeks, I wracked my brain figuring out what I could do that would change Strossmeyer's behavior. I worried about him as a student, and I worried about the effect he was having on my class. I was, without knowing it, treating myself as the subject who knows and Strossmeyer as the object to be controlled. While demanding that Strossmeyer be responsible for his own learning, I was only too happy to take control of his behavior.

I won't say that the course ended up on my list of "Best Ever." It did not. The class was still plagued with problems. It was full of students who were woefully unprepared academically and emotionally for a college-level course. Many of the students failed to read the material assigned in spite of daily quizzes and journal assignments. Some of the students discussed personal topics of interest rather than the assigned topics in their small groups, even though they had to make presentations to the class. Too many of the students dropped the course midsemester or failed. Yet I do think that there was a change in the class dynamic after the contract with Strossmeyer made it possible for interested students to gain something from the class and several reluctant students to become interested as the course progressed.

Now, at the beginning of each semester, I begin by explaining that I am interested in all students learning, but ultimately, students take control of their own learning. I also explain that the class must be an environment in which anyone who wishes to learn is allowed to do so. Personal conduct is also each student's responsibility. When students are disruptive in class, I sometimes still try to garner peer pressure. It often works. When it does not, however, I no longer lose sleep trying to figure out how to cope with the problem. I directly involve the student, who becomes the agent of his or her own authority.

Works Cited

Freire, Paulo. 1970. *Pedagogy of the Oppressed.* Trans. Myra Bergman Ramos. New York: Seabury P.

Foucault, Michel. 1995. *Discipline and Punish: The Birth of the Prison.* Trans. Alan Sheridan. 2nd ed. New York: Random House.

2

The Angry Student with the C+

Ann Dean

In my first semester as a composition teacher, I encountered several good-natured, hardworking, intelligent students whose writing did not significantly improve between September and December. One particular student in this group, Suzi, came to see me frequently in my office and in the café on campus. The café had a south-facing glass wall, and each week we both sweated with effort as the sun beat down on us, the paper, and the rickety little table. Suzi wrote with passion and framed her arguments as moral questions. Her third paper, for instance, was titled, "It's a Power Thing." I had asked the class to consider Stanley Fish's (2000) "How to Recognize a Poem When You See One," one of the pieces in David Bartholomae and Anthony Petrosky's (2000) anthology, *Ways of Reading.* In response to Fish's claims that "meanings, in the form of culturally derived interpretive categories, make readers," Suzi wrote:

> That is what disgusts me and I firmly disagree with Fish. I do not deny that I, myself, have been influenced by many people in my life; my parents, friends, teachers, and even Hollywood stars. But *I* will not be manipulated into believing what others want me to believe. As an *individual,* I have *the power* to choose what I will believe and what I won't.

As this passage makes clear, Suzi was a strong writer. She had ideas. She cared about her ideas. She wanted to do well in the class. Then and now, I would be thrilled if more of my students shared these characteristics.

Our problem developed when I tried to push Suzi toward the next step in college writing, those described in the "B" and "A" sections of the course's program-wide grading criteria: analysis, self-reflexivity, entering into and using the ideas in the reading. As Bartholomae and Petrosky put it in their introduction, "reading . . . can be the occasion for you to put things together, to notice this idea or theme rather than that one, to follow a writer's announced or secret ends while simultaneously following your own" (2000, p. 4). Suzi's response to Fish demonstrates that she did not see her reading this way at all, and that she did not understand her engagement with his essay in terms of putting things together, noticing patterns, following trails, or inventing paths. Instead, she saw Fish's argument as an attack on her status as an independent individual, someone with power. Her response was not to follow him down a new path, but to defend herself from his claims, and from the implication that she was a dupe of the media, her family, or her society.

My inability to understand Suzi's agonistic model of reading prevented me from building a bridge between her interpretive strategies and the new ones I hoped to teach her. When she and I talked about the draft of this paper, for instance, I saw the paragraph above as full of potential for further development, so I asked her a series of questions: "What is the difference between 'influence' and 'manipulation'?" "How do you know what an individual is?" "Where did the word 'individual' come from?" In response to each question, she pointed at a particular line of her draft, read it slowly aloud, and explained why it was important. As the semester passed, Suzi and I discussed almost every line of her writing this way, as I asked more and more questions and she hammered home her ideas both orally and in writing.

This tactic was a dismal failure. After our exhaustive and exhausting conversations, Suzi would turn in a final paper that wasn't significantly different from the draft we had discussed. I was mystified, and so was she. We both continued to work, increasingly frustrated and tense. In her fourth paper she wrote about her struggles with an eating disorder, her constant desire for perfection. She got angrier and angrier; I got guiltier and guiltier.

In December, when Suzi came to pick up her folder and her final C+ for the semester, she was on crutches. She'd fallen and injured her knee. Her eyes were filled with tears and a helpful friend carried her backpack and opened the door for her. Although her accident was entirely unrelated to my class, I had the distinct sensation that my terrible teaching had crippled this fine student. For weeks afterward, I ducked out of sight whenever I saw a woman on crutches.

The problem Suzi presented to me was both intellectual and emotional. To help her write better, I needed to understand that different models of reading, writing, and learning were operating in my class. And I needed to face up to an angry, passionate, combative person. But I could not learn what I needed to learn unless I was willing to look that anger in the face and ask myself what had caused it.

Such close observation and questioning are not my instinctive, gut responses to angry people. Usually I try a combination of placating friendliness and, as soon as possible, flight. These gut reactions, nice and encouraging though they made me, were counterproductive in Suzi's case. Because I was so distressed by her tension and so afraid of her resentment, I did not observe her writing closely, and I gave her conflicting messages. When she read aloud to me from her papers, filling in orally with further justifications of her positions, I would say, "That's wonderful! I think that will be great." I was imagining that in revision, Suzi would write a further paragraph analyzing, for instance, the difference between "influence" and "manipulation," using Fish's ideas about groups and interpretation. But what Suzi *heard* was "wonderful" and "great." So, I now think, she figured that that paragraph was okay the way it was, and that the elusive, mysterious problem with the paper must be elsewhere.

As a student myself, I had always returned to my own drafts, looking for the best parts, moving things around, finding holes in my arguments, rewriting sentences for better rhythm or greater clarity. I had developed this process from watching my mother, an MA student in English during my high school years, cut papers apart and tape them back together, making long streamers on the living-room floor. No teacher had ever taught me to revise. Thus, I did not have a professional language for talking with other people about a process I had experienced as the private, at-home part of writing.

Since then, I have read Nancy Sommers' (1980) "Revision Strategies of Student Writers and Experienced Adult Writers," in which Sommers argues that many students believe that "the meaning to be communicated is already there, already finished . . . ready to be communicated, and all that is necessary is a better word" (p. 47). Revision, for these students, involves finding a better word or perhaps a better word order for expressing the paper's main idea. Many students have never experienced or seen the steps that I watched my mother's papers go through on our living-room floor. Because I did not consciously know what I knew about revision, or how I had learned it, I assumed that these steps were an inherent part of writing.

My inability to be explicit about the standards and practices of academic writing are characteristic of the WASP culture of elite education, as Lisa Delpit (1996) explains. In this case, there was a difference between home culture and school culture for me, as well as for my students. The knowledge I had about writing from home was a cultural common sense, a practice rather than a theory, so it was particularly difficult for me to make it explicit. I imagined that Suzi had gone through those steps and come up dry, produced nothing. And if those steps had produced nothing, then I did not know what else to recommend.

What should you do when you try to write and you just . . . can't? That question was so frightening to me, both as a teacher and as a graduate student, that I could not face it. That was the problem I turned away from as I asked question after question in my conferences with Suzi and as I only half-listened to the answers, hoping that she would work them out in detail in writing, at home, alone. So, as I avoided Suzi's angry eyes, I avoided the question of what she was really doing in her writing, the question of what I needed to change in my teaching, and the question of what good academic writing really is and how it is done. And I developed a new habit of avoiding women on crutches.

So here is my advice about such situations: Find the angriest student in your class, look her in the eye, and ask her what she wants. Then give her something to write, watch her writing it, and read it as closely as you can. This is a very scary thing to do, both intellectually and emotionally, and I still sometimes find ways to get around my own knowledge that I must do it. Sometimes, however, I manage to pull it off. Looking back at Suzi's writing now, for instance, I can see that because she thought her ideas were in constant danger of "manipulation" from people like Fish (and me), and that her only salvation was, as the put it, "*the power* to choose what I will believe and what I won't," the class's grading criteria were a threat to her sense of her own rights as a student. In defense of her present understandings, she used all her writing skills to shore up her positions against the onslaught of new ideas, rather than to explore the new ideas and ask new and difficult questions. And when she changed her papers, she strengthened her positions—she worked even harder to make her points strongly, just as she did in our meetings as she pointed with her finger and read aloud. Her behavior and her writing both indicated her understanding of the goal of good writing: to win a fight in an agonistic arena among other finished and atomistic ideas.

Suzi was using the same group of rhetorical strategies in each paper, working harder and harder to do what she already knew how to do rather than trying something new. Or, as David Bartholomae puts it in "Inventing the University" (1985), "the writing is limited as much by a student's ability to imagine 'what might be said' as it is by cognitive control strategies" (p. 146). Had I been paying attention, I would have been able to see that pattern. But I was not. To revise Bartholomae's claim, the writing was limited as much by *the teacher's* ability to imagine "what might be said" as it was by the student's strategies. Neither Suzi nor I could see any alternative to the rhetorical forms and cultural practices of writing we were accustomed to. The limits on our imaginations produced those conversations that, instead of being real exchanges, were alternating repetitions of what we already knew. And the increasing emotional intensity of those conversations froze us even further into our positions.

In order to take up Lisa Delpit's (1996) invitation to clearly articulate the unwritten rules and unspoken standards of academic culture, it is necessary to be more explicit than I could, that first semester, imagine. I was teaching a course organized around revision; students wrote multiple drafts of each paper and each assignment asked students to return with a new perspective to a reading they had done earlier in the semester. The book's introduction described this recursive pattern, and I certainly told my students that revision was central to the writing process. But none of that mattered to this student, because she could not think of anything to write in her revision.

If I had understood this problem at the time, then, as a first-semester composition teacher, I would still have had the challenge of naming and describing an alternative idea of good writing, of finding examples of "what might be said," of giving Suzi and my other students a bridge to move across as they experimented with writing in these new ways. In Suzi's case, I would have had to prove to her that she would be safe and would gain something valuable if she at least momentarily let go of "*the power*" she had found in the rhetorical strategies she already knew.

I don't particularly like having to figure out new things on my feet at the spur of the moment in front of twenty people. I had entered a PhD program in literature because I like to go off and think about the same thing for years and then write and rewrite before I show anyone my ideas. And so my effort to work with Suzi and her classmates would have been imperfect, experimental, uncomfortable. These were compelling reasons for avoiding Suzi's eyes.

However, like my students, I can figure out things I don't already know. I can watch students writing, ask them what they think, listen to their answers, and give them experience with new ideas and new ways of working with ideas. And that is why teaching composition is an intellectual project, as well as a Herculean labor and a psychological challenge. Like literary criticism, composition teaching is interpretive. As composition teachers, we listen and read closely, ask questions to which even we won't be comfortable with the answers, meet our students' eyes, and look for patterns, for names, for meaning.

I want to note here that other kinds of anger also surface in freshman composition, especially for teachers who work with expressive writing and personal experience. If you really feel in danger from a student's anger, you should not ignore that feeling. Do not meet with such a student in a remote office; do not close the door. Meet in a café, or with an administrator or fellow instructor present. Do tell someone, preferably in writing, if you feel threatened by a student. If a student herself seems in danger from her own anger, you should notify an administrator or someone from your school's counseling service. It is good to remember, too, that you are the teacher, and that students have at least twelve years of experience with teachers behind them when they get to you. Some of those teachers may well have been unfair, or mean, or bored, or racist. So a student may assume that you are unfair, or mean, or bored, or racist, no matter what you do. Similarly, not every college student is a very nice person. You may get one of the less nice ones, and you have to protect yourself even as you do your best to carry out your job of teaching that student to write.

But Suzi *was* a nice student, and also bright and hardworking. She was practicing all the skills of being a good student she had learned in high school: She wasn't afraid to ask for help; she was openly aiming for the best possible grade; she was serious about school. The failure, in other words, was mine.

I know now that angry students direct me toward questions that can improve my teaching the most. I can always learn from the justified anger of a student who comes to class willing to work, but who can't figure out what work to do. That student brings experience different from mine into the classroom. If I can ignore my own urges to back off and placate her, then I can step forward to look closely. Her anger, which threatens to reveal my own ignorance and confusion, also promises to reveal her ideas, and to teach us both something that we did not know before.

12   Ann Dean

Works Cited

Bartholomae, David. 1985. "Inventing the University." In *When A Writer Can't Write,* edited by Mike Rose, 134–162. New York: Guilford Press.

———— and Anthony Petrosky. 2000. *Ways of Reading: An Anthology for Writers,* 5th edition. New York: Bedford St. Martin's.

Delpit, Lisa. 1996. *Other People's Children: Cultural Conflict in the Classroom.* New York: New Press.

Fish, Stanley. 2000. "How to Recognize a Poem When You See One." *Ways of Reading: An Anthology for Writers,* 3rd ed., edited by David Bartholomae and Anthony Petrosky, 139–155. New York: Bedford St. Martin's.

Sommers, Nancy. 1997. "Revision Strategies of Student Writers and Experienced Adult Writers." CCC, v 31, n 4: 378–388.

3

Wielding Authority in a Nonauthoritarian Classroom

Victoria Arthur

Given the dire outlook on the job market for English instructors, I'm thrilled when I receive a job offer to teach English 100 at the local community college immediately after earning my Master's. For the first time, I'm going to be a bona fide professional, no longer negotiating the liminal state of student/ instructor in the comparative safety of a structured composition program. But I'm still in an inherently tenuous position—a part-time, temporary adjunct on a quarterly contract. I can't survive on part-time income, so, like many of my underemployed colleagues, I also pick up courses to teach at another community college thirty miles down the freeway. A core of permanent part-timers round out the department's limited faculty, but every quarter, new faces come and go in the single office I end up sharing with four to six other transient instructors (and this is a vast improvement from the other community college that provides a break room for adjuncts' office space).

The student population at the community college is different from what I'm used to at the Tier II University where I was a TA. Now I have a mix of college-age students who choose not to attend a four-year school for a variety of reasons (financial, academic, personal), a few high-performing returning older adults and, most surprising to me, a large complement of high school students via the Running Start program. I quickly discover that Running Start allows high school juniors and seniors to earn college credits, at the state's expense, by attending community college for part of the school day. My initial assumption is that these must be the most motivated and qualified students; I soon learn otherwise. Because the program does not impose any acceptance criteria, students self-select to participate. Therefore, some Running Start students consider their time on campus more of an escape from the high school scene than a chance to focus on college-level learning.

A large number of Running Start students place into English 100, the gateway course to college credit English 101. This course had undergone major curricular and philosophical changes in the previous two years, moving in a direction that matches my training. The pedagogical model had shifted from counting grammatical errors as a way to judge writing ability, to attempting to encourage and evaluate an amorphous element called "critical thinking." I feel right at home with the challenges of this approach, as I had spent the past two years immersed in the concept that writing is a way to *make* knowledge, to come to deeper understanding, to develop "earned insights" about the world and oneself, courtesy of my training with Donna J. Qualley, Director of Composition at Western Washington University. Symbolic of this commitment to critical thinking, Qualley had renamed English 101 "Writing and Critical Inquiry" to reflect this approach. The new and improved English 100 at the community college was committed to a similar focus—moving students from writing "clean, but vacuous" essays (no substance, but also no errors) to potentially messier, but more thoughtful and complex essays. My training and teaching experience enabled me to be an active agent of such change.

I enter my first class ready to offer the students (what I consider) an exciting opportunity to become critical thinkers, and I end up with a classroom half full of Running Start high schoolers. I am not impugning high school students as a group—some of them are engaged and add to the class and others don't, just as with any student population—but the wide range of maturity levels and degrees of commitment to college-level learning led to a disjuncture of expectations between me and one student in particular.

Rick (not his real name) immediately becomes the dominant force in the classroom. I appreciate that he consistently speaks up in class and helps to get discussions started. But he also automatically answers every single question posed to the class, never allowing any other, less vocal, students a chance to speak. (Other students do not even try to speak after a short time, knowing that Rick will always come to the class' rescue.) Rick turns out to be talkative and opinionated. His strongly held ideas about composition are useful for starting a dialogue with the perspectives I present, which is beneficial for students to come to their own understanding instead of passively accepting my ready-made knowledge.

Before long, however, it becomes clear that Rick's opinions are so inflexible that he is not open to receiving new ideas at all. He quickly devolves into the kind of resistant student we've all had experience with—students who don't want to be in a required class, students who have decided they already know what the class is going to teach, students who are downright antagonistic toward new ideas. Rick becomes all that and more—resistant, argumentative, disrespectful and, I'm sorry to say, downright irritating. Whatever I teach, he has already learned it, the *right* way. If I introduce an idea different from what he had learned in high school, he responds by denigrating my variation as simply a matter of opinion. When I ask the class a question, he argues against the validity of my question, my presentation of information—in short, my authority as a teacher.

This situation erupts one day when he insists that the grammatical question we are discussing is "just a matter of opinion," a phrase he repeats three times, with increasing agitation, before he slams his hand out face down and opens a textbook for another class, pointedly dismissing the topic. I am stunned by the rudeness and inappropriateness of his behavior and become immediately incensed. I feel like I've been challenged; he has thrown down the gauntlet and I must respond. Somehow between the two of us we've created a power struggle that I feel required to win, at all costs. Until now, I cannot imagine myself asking a student to leave the classroom, but here is Rick, seeming to demand that I deal with him on *his* terms—prove that I can dominate him or cede control of the classroom to him. My body is coursing with adrenaline at the conflict.

As I recount this event, the "coursing adrenaline" seems a bit extreme, even to me. But at the time, that is really how I felt. It felt like a career-ending challenge to me, my authority, my ability to help anyone learn anything. Although I dislike conflict, I felt obligated to demonstrate, both to him, and maybe even more importantly to his classmates, that *I* was in charge of that classroom.

But wait—how did we get to this impasse? I can't even believe that is me I just described in the last paragraph. Rick's behavior and my response do not fit with anything I think I know about myself or how I want to teach. I thought I wanted to allow my students to have authority, in their texts and in the classroom, not wield it myself. I had been highly influenced by Peter Elbow's (1997) and Donald Murray's (1997) approaches to writing as process, and Kenneth Bruffee's (1997) theories about collaboration and social constructionism. I am convinced that the key to managing one's writing process most effectively is to become aware of it. And only the student can become an expert in his or her own writing process; as a teacher, all I can do is offer tasks and ask questions that lead them in the direction of self-discovery. And because academic discourse is the construction of a particular language community, to quote Kenneth Bruffee (1997), my authority comes from "being a certified representative of the communities of knowledgeable peers that students aspire to join" (p. 409). As a fluent member of the academic discourse community, I am able to provide feedback on adherence to academic conventions, but the students are experts on how to get from where they are to where "the academy" wants them to be. And I take to heart the axiom of collaboration that novices learn best how to accomplish a new task from working with others at their same skill level. (They learn information best from an expert, but putting knowledge in practice is best done with peers).

All of these pedagogical strands wind around the central issue of student as authority. I try to encourage students to become experts on their own writing process by assigning reflective letters and essays. I encourage them to see each other as resources in assigning peer critiques and small group exercises. I consciously identify academic discourse as a "truth" (one of many) as defined by one particular language community, not the Truth (the only one) about good writing, period. I welcome the truths that students bring with them from other language communities that are not usually valued in a college setting by assigning Amy Tan's

(1990, 1998) "Mother Tongue" and a writing prompt in which the student writer is the expert explaining their various Englishes to me.

And right out of all this student-centeredness comes the desire to assert my teacherly authority: I am peripherally aware of the rest of the class waiting in breathless silence as I focus intently on Rick. I only have a moment to consider my course of action. I calmly ask him to do his homework for another class somewhere other than my English class. After the obligatory stare-down, he slams his books into his book bag and stalks out of the room, heading off to complain to somebody about my unfair treatment, I am sure. After class I returned to my office to recover from what had felt like a physical confrontation and figure out what the heck just happened. I realize that I've just experienced the contradiction of attempting to authorize my students while maintaining enough authority to manage a classroom: I'm smack dab in the middle of the difficulty of creating an egalitarian atmosphere as described by Paulo Friere (1999) in the 1970s.

I felt I was doing the right thing for my students in allowing them space to disagree, with each other *and* with me, and come to their own sense of ownership about the information, techniques, and strategies I present. I want all of my students to get a sense of their own voice and feel powerful enough to use it. But as I replayed the important exchanges of the quarter, I realized that I had been fearful of reining Rick in because I didn't want to be perceived as authoritarian by the other students. I thought any display of authority on my part would silence *all* of the students, which was the direct opposite of my goal as a teacher. Without realizing it, I had come to equate any show of authority with being *authoritarian*. Therefore, the need to demonstrate my authority as a teacher felt like a failure of my student-centered approach.

I wonder how I came to have such distrust in my ability to use authority effectively. I don't think it's solely my pedagogical training, however, but also my experiences as a student (and perhaps my gender?). I was a very successful student, as most graduate students probably are. I was adept at interpreting what teachers wanted and delivering it to them. I have come to define this as the "good girl" phenomenon (although I'm sure a version of it happens for boys also). I truly enjoyed pleasing teachers by paying attention, making eye contact, and responding with positive body language during lectures. Favorable comments on exams and essays would make me beam with pride at having fulfilled teachers' expectations. Even to myself, I sound like a suck-up, but I received a lot of satisfaction from complying with authority. I see now that I identified with the authority of teacher from a very early age. I honored the role of teacher almost regardless of the characteristics of the individual at the front of the room. I accepted the authority of the role without any explicit display of power. And I guess I assumed I could be that same kind of teacher—receiving the benefits of the authority inherent in the position of teacher, without having to prove my authority as an individual person. Nothing in my own academic experience prepared me for Rick's hostile approach to my attempt at giving students authority.

As a brand-new instructor, I (naively) didn't expect that some students want, like, and perhaps even need, the standard authoritative teacher. I guess I assumed that by the time students were in a college setting they would have explicitly chosen to be there (instead of being legally and traditionally bound to public school attendance) and would appreciate and gladly accept the responsibility for their own education that this type of approach requires. I even expected the ones who had trouble accepting the idea would be intellectually mature and sophisticated enough to perceive its advantages to them as learners. Admittedly, this is rather narrow-minded and based on experience with only a certain type of student. It posits a high level of flexibility on the part of students from a wide variety of backgrounds. Perhaps it is an accurate description of white, middle-class students who see themselves as having power in many aspects of their lives and as consistently capable of academic success (like the majority of students I taught at the state university), but that doesn't mean it is workable for all students.

So, once I accepted the fact that my approach privileged a certain type of student, I had to start thinking about which students found it yet another academic obstacle. Students raised in authoritarian households, enculturated to looking outward for approval, would probably have difficulty. Also, students who perceive education as a process of transmission, where the teacher is the holder of knowledge and "pours" it into passive students vessels to "fill" them up, may have a problem valuing the opinions of other students, whom they see as not knowing anything more than they do, and become frustrated by the teacher they perceive is "holding back" the real answers. Another type of student, who sees school solely as a gateway to economic opportunity and is in school for the pragmatic reason of getting a good, well-paying job, may tend to focus on education for what it offers them in the "real" world, and perceive a diploma as a ticket to increased opportunity, ignoring, or simply not having the time and energy for the personal enrichment potential of higher education. Of course, these are simplistic descriptions and nonexclusive distinctions; many students exhibit various strains of authoritarian thinking for more reasons than I have outlined here. But the importance of my thinking moving in this direction is the importance of seeing valid reasons for smart, hard-working students not to embrace my philosophy. It takes the onus off their "unsophisticated" level of intelligence or maturity, and forces me to see that the diversity of backgrounds, values, and reasons for participating in higher education are a meaningful distinction I need to take into account as a teacher. Granted, this is a rather obvious insight, and one may argue that I should already have been aware of it. On an intellectual level, I *was* already aware of it—but the benefit of the conflict and my reflection on it is that the intellectual knowledge becomes working knowledge—an earned insight that is truly mine and not just borrowed from an outside authority (the kind I would like my students to have).

The discussion so far assumes that my student-centered approach was successful in empowering my students and Rick just didn't understand his new role. But was he misunderstanding the issues of authority in the classroom, or was I? I postured as if I were not the authority of the classroom, but when Rick became resistant, I still wanted to have the authority to make him accept my "truth." I'm afraid that at that early stage in my teaching career (I feel I have to make some defense of myself), I was comfortable being student-centered only when the student tacitly accepted my disguised teacherly authority.

But I could only disguise my authority to myself with the kind of student that accepted it and played their role of respectful, interested student (the kind of student I was). Rick was calling me on the issue of authority that I was trying to ignore—the very paradox of my philosophy. As Bruffee (1997) reminds us, after outlining the many benefits of the teacher trying to resist defining their students' truth for them, when it comes down to it, it is an artificial release of authority. It made me feel good to try to help my students become experts on their own writing, but none of them ever lost sight of who had the real control. As the teacher, I could not escape from the power of being the final arbiter of grades, the currency of the institution, however much I tried. In many ways, I was the naive one, trying to create an atmosphere at odds with the greater academic culture. I'd tried to ignore the realities of the situation that the students saw clearly.

As Rick storms out of the classroom, I turn my attention back to the rest of the class, who have faded to the periphery during my experience of the intensity of the conflict. I expect that the rest of the students will align themselves with Rick as the maligned student and against me as the mean teacher, and am emotionally girding myself for continued strife and bad attitude. I swing right back into the discussion we had been having and immediately feel a different atmosphere. To my surprise, it is lighter, happier, more open, friendlier. Before that day, only two students spoke regularly in class, Rick and a bright female student. During the rest of that class session, about eight more students speak, six of them who had never spoken in class without being called on before. And it wasn't out of fear; it was more out of solidarity. It was as if they wanted to show that they were on my side. I'm not sure if my display of authority had gained their respect or made them feel protected from an intellectual bully, but they seemed to go out of their way to reward me by their willing participation.

But what about Rick? I was expecting that this was now going to become a major to-do; he would complain to administration and I would have to defend my actions. I immediately document the situation back at my office after class (which is always a good idea in a situation that may escalate). I couldn't have been more wrong. Don't get me wrong, he didn't turn into a model student overnight. I am still unsure about his level of maturity for success in college classes and was glad to see him pass my class and move on, but something happened that I completely didn't expect. He became respectful. Or at least he performed the external behaviors of respect. I don't think he accepted any more of what I was saying than before, but he would raise his hand in class, call me Ms. Arthur (I generally go by Victoria with students) and made a show of respect.

Surprisingly to me, he seemed much more comfortable with his position in the class (and mine) after the conflict. I was troubled by the need for such an explicit display of authority on my part, but he seemed glad to have been "put in his place." He wanted to know who the top dog was, and now that he knew, he knew how to act. He was pushing the boundaries of acceptable behavior to find out just how far he could go. But he didn't really want the power he was attempting to exert. I think he, and possibly the rest of the class, felt nervous as long as he could challenge me in an antagonistic way. He perceived my lack of obvious authoritarianism as a power vacuum, one that in his discomfort he attempted to fill. I didn't realize that his acting out was a hidden request for me to act like what he considered a teacher, so he could be the student.

In thinking about the conflict now, I see it much more as a conflict within me than one with a student. I thought I was giving students power, but I wasn't willing to admit the power I really did have in that institutional setting. I think the biggest lesson that I have learned from Rick is to be honest with myself and my students about the balance of power in my classroom. I still strive to be student-centered (and am probably more genuinely student-centered now than I was with this class), but I try to create possibilities for students to gain power in ways that jive with the context of the academic setting. While I still encourage my students to start seeing themselves and their peers as experts by requiring peer feedback, providing revision-oriented feedback (instead of grades) on drafts, lurking in threaded discussions, and assigning student presentations (so students guide each other in learning), I no longer deny the institutional power I inherently wield. In clearly identifying the various roles I play as teacher—coach, guide, referee, evaluator—I help students identify and cope with their shifting roles.

Works Cited

Bruffee, Kenneth. 1984. "Collaborative Learning and the 'Conversation of Mankind.'" *College English* 46.7: 635–52. Rpt. In *Cross-Talk in Composition Theory: A Reader,* edited by Victor Villanueva, 393–414. Urbana: NCTE.

Elbow, Peter. 1991. "Reflections on Academic Discourse: How It Relates to Freshmen and Colleagues," *College English* 53:2: 135–55.

Freire, Paulo. 1999. *Pedagogy of the Oppressed.* Trans. Myra Bergman Ramos. New York: Continuum.

Murray, Donald. 1992. *Learning by Teaching.* Portsmouth: Boynton Cook.

———. 1997. "Teach Writing as a Process Not Product." In *Cross-Talk in Composition Theory,* edited by Victor Villanueva, Urbana: NCTE. 3–6.

Qualley, Donna. 1997. *Turns of Thought: Teaching Composition as Reflexive Inquiry.* Portsmouth: Boynton/Cook Heinemann.

Tan, Amy. 1998. "Mother Tongue." In *Fields of Reading: Motives for Writing,* edited by Nancy R. Comley, David Hamilton, Carl H. Klauss, Robert Scholes, Nancy Sommers 5th ed. New York: St. Martin's Press. Reprinted from *Threepenny Review* (1990) 315–320. Title appears "Under Western Eyes" in that version.

4

The Unwelcome Rhetor in Our Midst

Brad Peters

When younger writing instructors discover the joys of why their senior colleagues decided to teach writing in the first place, we all drink new wine and grow tipsy with excitement. But when younger teachers also discover the classroom realities that test those joys, we have to share our buried frustrations as well. For instance, if we're haunted by the memories of a rare but disconcerting student who has successfully undermined our pedagogical aims, it may turn out that our younger colleagues need us to exhume those old, restive bones.

I can still feel the first rush of enthusiasm that emanated from a teaching associate I'll call "Judy," as she completed a preservice seminar in writing instruction with me. She eagerly anticipated a classroom where she would guide students to participate in the shared authority of Bruffee's (1996) collaborative learning, introduce them to the ethical conception of Ede's and Lunsford's (1996) invoked audience, engage them with the coded discourse of Bartholomae's (1996) invented university. She would do so not by privileging the consensus that some feminist pedagogy requires, but by asserting the feminist perspective that "It is more productive to bring out and examine the contradictions and conflicts" that her students would already maintain as members of communities and groups that inhabited both marginal and dominant positions (see Jarratt, 1991, p. 116). In other words, Judy was not naive about the challenges she would find in her classroom. She felt that "the structures of this society (government, justice system, educational system, media, etc.) are rooted in fundamentally racist, sexist, homophobic ideas. . . . I just imagine class discussions on these kinds of issues to be fiery sometimes"— and she saw class activities as a way to give her students practice in acquitting themselves well when faced with the everyday confrontations of living in an urban area deeply divided along racial, cultural, and economic lines.

For the first year that Judy taught, she seemed to be doing precisely what she'd set out to do, placing the practice of *dissoi logoi* (conflicting views about

Greenbaum (2001) identifies as a-dialogical, "verbal aggression": attacks characterized by hostility and directed at one individual—me (p. 160).

Still, as I recalled that semester with Gary, Judy observed that her student, too, was making her improve her classroom strategies. But the harder she worked, the more her troublemaker got others to find fault. "Yep," I agreed. "In my case, I sent everyone the message that Gary and I were competing for control." I could see how much power I had given to Gary, how unlike a forum our class had become, and how uneasy it made the other students feel. My goal, teaching rhetoric as a dialogue, had derailed.

The situation came to a head after midterm. Although I had resolutely defended writing as a dialogue, I had left grades out of that dialogue. Accordingly, I asked the class to grade themselves. Students should focus on three components of the course—reading, writing, speaking—and explain what grades they felt they'd earned in each. I announced that students who justified their grades with specific examples, strong reasoning, logical organization, consistent focus, and detailed development usually demonstrated the same qualities in their overall work—so their self-assigned grades were often accurate.

I should have anticipated that Gary would give himself an "A" and urge everyone else to do the same. Not everyone followed his lead, but I had to "correct" lots of inflated grades. When I returned the self-evaluations, many students reacted as if I'd betrayed them. Gary used this reaction to stunning effect. The class turned into a hive of angry wasps. Suddenly everything was wrong with the course: the exercises, the syllabus, the texts, the assignments, the workload. The students spoiled for a showdown.

Thinking quickly, I told them to take out a sheet of paper and explain what they felt were the major problems, as well as the most acceptable aspects of the class. "You need to provide me with a balanced, persuasive document," I said. After setting up that context, I said they needed to give me some recommendations. Then I hesitated for a moment. Should I stay and respond to the recommendations after they finished writing them? Should we all battle it out? If I weren't present to conduct our dialogue, wouldn't Gary dominate it? Who would speak, besides him? Who would remain silent? I recalled Susan Jarratt's (1991) warnings that "we can't always control the ways discursive power works in our classes. . . . We can't always undo the institutional authority of our roles through our instructions and assurances" (p. 111).

I told everyone I would leave the classroom while they held a "town meeting." They should elect a moderator to assure that everyone—and I stressed *every one of them*—had a say. A recording secretary should sum up the conversation. When they finished, a class representative should bring the proceedings to my office. I said I'd come to the next class session with a response. Then I left.

Although I expected Gary to come to my office, one of the quietest students in class—Alec—showed up instead. Gary had started out moderating the meeting, Alec said, "But Gary just wanted everyone to list complaints. I told them we had to say some good stuff, too, or you'd blow us off." I glanced over the meeting's minutes and noticed an intelligent balance of objections, compliments, and suggestions. "We had a pretty good discussion," Alec told me. "It was the first time this semester we've all had a chance to talk. Most of us are still mad, but we liked it."

I mulled over Alec's words. Who was the real base rhetorician in our class? Gary—*or me?* For all of my emphasis on dialogue, I suddenly realized that most of the talk in our class consisted of *me* justifying the reasons we were doing some activity, *me* setting up the parameters of how I wanted the students to react, *me* addressing what I knew were Gary's complaints, but what I assumed were everyone else's complaints, as well. Accordingly, I had developed the practice of acknowledging only one voice in class—*the a-dialogical voice of the person who resisted me most.* It was only at a moment of collective confrontation that I realized I had to meet the results of Gary's counterresistance with what Elizabeth Flynn (2001) calls "strategic resistance": a model of how people can form coalitions to express what they want or need in an oppressive situation. Building on Dale Bauer's and Katharine Rhoades' (1996) observations, Flynn (2001) advocates "constructing a classroom climate and curriculum which allows students to generate questions fueling the course"—and she says that such "*Dialogical* teaching also involves establishing common ground with students . . . to negotiate the private–public split" that counterresistance often creates (p. 25; emphasis mine).

Two days later, I returned to class with a grading policy and a list of ten concrete steps for improving grades. I told the students I would often refer to the town meeting minutes to figure out ways to give everyone a chance to have more of a say. Even though I didn't agree with every suggestion or objection they had provided, I saw the reasoning in each. I would therefore make an effort to address the suggestions that I didn't think would compromise their learning—and I would consult with them along the way, to see if they thought I should modify anything further. As we went forward, their most often-repeated suggestion was to clarify the criteria by which I'd be evaluating them in every assignment, so they pressured me to develop rubrics that would guide them toward revising. It's a practice I continue to this day. To my surprise, this action put an end to my contest with Gary and established something of the dialogue I'd touted. I just hadn't expected the dialogue to become focused on my pedagogy. Yet how blind I was not to see that the way students perceive our pedagogy is often the one true indication of what we're *really* doing.

At the end of my story, Judy looked at me skeptically. "I don't think I can turn things around the way you did. I'm a woman; students react differently to me."

Maybe, I replied. But I told her she was also a savvier pedagogue than I had been. "The important changes happened after I convinced students that they really did have a voice," I observed. "Can you do the same?"

In asking this question, I also wondered out loud if Judy could provide a model of persuasion, not necessarily in the way I'd done with my own class, but in some way that displayed strategic behavior that the quiet students—especially the women in her class—would see how to mirror (see Greenbaum, 2001, p. 161)? Maybe, I ventured, the best way to deal with counterresistance in any class is to give the ones who are silenced by it an ongoing, structured opportunity to speak back.

Judy paused for a moment. "Maybe," she sighed. "But what about the students who will lose out if I do something wrong?"

Judy had a valid point. I told her that whatever she decided, I would support her. Then I shared with her a journal entry that a student wrote in Gary's class, shortly after their "town meeting." I asked the student for permission to reproduce it, and I've included her words in almost every undergraduate syllabus I've taught since that experience. The student wrote:

> Today I think I figured out what this class is all about.
>
> It's about opinions and facts. It's about analyzing, judging, introspection, understanding, arguing, agreeing, and a hundred other things.
>
> It's interesting.
>
> It's discovering, maybe giving up old views.
>
> Anything dealing with reading and writing involves a more personal involvement. In this class we learn that writing can be unexpected self-discovery. When reading, we learn that part of what we bring into a book we get out of it, and our view isn't the only view.
>
> This class is an open forum. We learn about as much from each other as the books.
>
> We can persuade others of our view or be persuaded or just sit back and listen. This class is a lot more personal than I expected.

I still believe that fewer students lose out than we think whenever we teach them about rhetoric—and then give them the genuine occasions to practice it.

Works Cited

Bartholomae, David. 1996. "Inventing the University." In *Composition in Four Keys: Inquiring into the Field,* edited by Mark Wiley, Barbara Gleason, and Louise Wetherbee Phelps, 460–79. Mountain View, CA: Mayfield Publishing Company.

Bauer, Dale, and Katharine Rhoades. 1996. "The Meanings and Metaphors of Student Resistance." In *Antifeminism in the Academy,* edited by VeVe Clark, Shirley Nelson Garner, Margaret Higgonet, and Ketu Katrak, 95–113. New York: Routledge.

Bruffee, Kenneth. 1996. "Collaborative Learning and the 'Conversation of Mankind.'" In *Composition in Four Keys: Inquiring into the Field,* edited by Mark Wiley, Barbara Gleason, and Louise Wetherbee Phelps, 84–97. Mountain View, CA: Mayfield Publishing Company.

Ede, Lisa, and Andrea Lunsford. 1996. "Audience Addressed/Audience Invoked: The Role of Audience in Composition Theory and Pedagogy." In *Composition in Four Keys: Inquiring into the Field,* edited by Mark Wiley, Barbara Gleason, and Louise Wetherbee Phelps, 198–210. Mountain View, CA: Mayfield Publishing Company.

Flynn, Elizabeth. 2001. "Strategic, Counter-Strategic, and Reactive Resistance in the Feminist Classroom." In *Insurrections: Approaches to Resistance in Composition Studies,* edited by Andrea Greenbaum, 17–34. Albany, NY: State University of New York Press.

Greenbaum, Andrea. 2001. "'Bitch' Pedagogy: Agonistic Discourse and the Politics of Resistance." In *Insurrections: Approaches to Resistance in Composition Studies,* edited by Andrea Greenbaum, 151–68. Albany, NY: State University of New York Press.

Jarratt, Susan. 1991. "Feminism and Composition: The Case for Conflict." In *Contending with Words: Composition and Rhetoric in a Postmodern Age,* edited by Patricia Harkin and John Schilb, 105–23. New York: Modern Language Association of America.

Weaver, Richard. 1985. *The Ethics of Rhetoric.* Davis, CA: Hermagoras Press.

5

When Underlife Takes Over

An Insight on Student Resistance and Classroom Dynamics

Suzanne Diamond

In 1987, Robert Brooke borrowed the sociological concept of "underlife" in order to analyze disruptive classroom behaviors, both the kinds that make us uncomfortable and the kinds we presumably incite. In an article titled "Underlife and Writing Instruction," Brooke builds on Erving Goffman's (1961, 1963) work in order to define underlife as "the range of activities people develop to distance themselves from the surrounding institution" (p. 141).[1] Brooke explains that:

> In sociological theory, "underlife" refers to those behaviors which undercut the roles expected of participants in a situation—the ways an employee, for example, shows she is not just an employee, but has a more complex personality outside that role. (p. 141)

Clearly "underlife" is a direct kin of "resistance" in the classroom, the behaviors denoted by each being often a welcome facet of any dynamic social environment. Underlife, applied to classroom activity, is as likely to be productive as it is to be disruptive, as Brooke himself demonstrates:

> On the one hand, students disobey, write letters instead of taking notes, and whisper with their peers to show they are more than just students and can think independently of classroom expectations. On the other, writing teachers develop workshop methods, use small groups, and focus on students' own "voices" in order to help students see themselves as writers first and students second. (p. 141)

---

1. For other useful articles on underlife in the classroom, see also Worth Anderson, et al., "Cross-Curricular Underlife: A Collaborative Report on Ways with Academic Words," *College Composition and Communication* 41.1 (1990): 11–36.

Brooke underscores that both of these are underlife behaviors, one student initiated and one teacher initiated, even if the course-related motivations of each variation differ.[2]

The kinds of student underlife Brooke mentions—the letter-writing and whispering, for instance—can constitute a mild distraction in the classroom, but all in all, they comprise a benign nuisance at best. I would argue that it is the teacher-sanctioned underlife that merits greater attention. Brooke, like so many other proponents of radical pedagogy whose aims are as noble as their stances are, sadly, naive, fails to acknowledge that underlife can take far more vocal forms, that part of what students may elect to define themselves against is precisely our insistence that they "see themselves as writers first and students second." As employees and inevitable agents of academic institutions, in fact, we often amount to proximate representatives of the "surrounding institution" from which resistant members must work to "distance themselves." Creatively resistant students function to teach us something important if slightly dispiriting: that you do not step free of institutional authority simply by siding with its disenfranchised members. It does not please me to observe this, for the indictment extends to me as well; however, you do not become a radical by wearing blue jeans to school and sitting everybody in a circle.

I step forth timidly to argue that sometimes sincerity with our students dictates that we forgo the flattering images of ourselves and *inhabit* the authority we represent in our classrooms. We do our best work for people, I would suggest, precisely when we acknowledge our own compromised positions. What we can do, compromised although we are in terms of our own cultural resistance, is to model responsible ways of *using* social privilege. Searches after origins are often bound to be futile, and I believe this is true in the quest to know definitively how and why students resist; it is in our responses, I maintain, that we can be most effective. Whereas a teacher might only speculate on the possible root *causes* of student resistance, that same teacher's *response* to more difficult forms of resistance can make a huge difference in classroom functioning.

My vehemence about redirecting the conversation about student resistance grows out of a weird experience I once had some eleven years ago. When I was a graduate teaching assistant and in my second year in this role at Rutgers University, I taught a summer evening course whose classroom dynamic, from its earliest days, was underlife emerging into course content, largely at the hands of one very vocal student. Daily, I winced against the approaching evenings as I prepared the first few weeks' sessions. I worried about the challenge this strange dynamic itself posed to my willed self-image as a capable professional-in-training. I hope to remind teachers experiencing anything that resembles the chain of events I plan to recount that taking time to consider key factors in

---

2. One of Brooke's central claims, based on classroom research, is that students' in-class underlife behaviors are often more course-related than instructors might assume.

classroom group dynamics can bring the much needed poise, generosity, and effectiveness you may need to respond to resistance constructively.

To any teacher who has dealt uncomfortably with individual student resistance in the classroom setting—particularly a kind of resistance that begins to feel like out-and-out heckling—I would offer the following observation: First, become closely attentive to *your own* responses to the "resistance events" themselves. If you are like me, some of your anxiety in response to a resisting student stems not strictly from your reluctance to be drawn into a distraction or irrelevant harangue, but also from a basic uncertainty about where the *larger group stands* with regard to the verbally resistant student's issues of contention.

In this age of freak theater—the shouting-match talk shows and the radio tirades that pass for political commentary, for instance—it can be difficult to trust in the innate sense of fair play possessed by your classroom audience. In a difficult classroom encounter, it might not be so absurd to ask yourself, at least momentarily: Is the "resistor" *detracting* from the group experience or perhaps *advancing* the misgivings of a silent constituency, or even, more perversely, simply entertaining a *bored* constituency? If the resistor's demeanor toward you is sarcastic or dismissive, you might worry that her stance is just the leading edge of a more general backlash against the authority you inevitably represent (regardless of the scrupulous reluctance with which you assume it) in your course.

These anxieties, I suggest, are often unfounded, especially if you yourself are using your own institutional privilege to ensure a climate of fair play. Experience leads me to contend that so long as you maintain rigorously a courteous and respectful stance—*even, if not especially, toward a student whose demeanor toward you might be neither*—you can usually take comfort in the fact that the class, as a whole, is on the side of a functioning and cooperative environment; in other words, the group will be on *your* side in a difficult harangue so long as you maintain your own posture as an instructor who will *never* respond in kind to disrespectful behavior. On paper, this adage might sound trite; in certain kinds of classroom confrontations, however, I believe that maintaining this policy is the hardest work of teaching.

Emphatically, the best teaching openly invites student contention about course-related matters, even while it models the ways that respectful contention might take place. But respect for others' experiences, for their honor within the group, and for their personal legitimacy as meaning makers must flow in all directions, not only from teacher to student but also from student to other student and, yes, from student to teacher. I think that beginning teachers almost instinctively affirm that *students* deserve this kind of honor; so many of us are in teaching precisely to "right the wrongs" of a traditional pedagogy that presumably sanctioned bullying teachers. I think it is important also, however, that we bear in mind not only that a teacher, too, is entitled to respect and honor, but also that, because of her institutional authority (her politics notwithstanding), a teacher is best positioned to *model it precisely in adverse classroom conditions.*

As I have said, I myself learned this important lesson on the job; in the summer of 1990, as I began that second year as a teaching assistant, I perceived right away that there was a student in the class who was going to require considered management in the classroom. His name was "Danny," and there were several occasions during just the first two weeks of this summer course when his highly performative resistance in the classroom was a challenge verging on embarrassment—besides being a worry—to me; he would shout things out; state sweeping and sarcastic, yet "surfacy" positions *about* our readings that seemed not to be grounded *in* these readings; and leave the room and return without notice or explanation.

But these occasions reached their culmination in an evening when his behavior and my own *accidentally correct* response to it taught me a "lesson" about responding to resistance that I wish to offer my reader. On this evening, Danny showed up for class in unusual form, even by his own remarkable standard, and also, as I soon detected, without having done the required reading. Periodically, I quiz classes engaged in extended readings (we were covering a novel), and on this evening I had planned such a quiz.[3] Danny shifted visibly in his seat that evening and several times requested that I repeat different quiz questions for him, some of them several times.[4] He made these repeat requests in various orders; first could I repeat question seven, for instance, then question two. Let me caution my reader against pity here (for him *or* me): He was clearly intent on mischief. Then, about five minutes before the class would have submitted the quizzes, he called out loudly that he needed the rest room. Global policies are made to be broken, I am sure, but I have always maintained one; I never stand between any human being and a restroom. I assented, and the class and I waited for Danny to return before I announced that I would collect the short quizzes.

At this point, Danny yelled that he needed much more time, that he had only written down the quiz *questions,* and that he just now had only begun answering them. By now we were about twenty minutes into a two-and-a-half-hour evening class; everyone else had finished five or more minutes earlier. It was abundantly clear that a liberal amount of time had transpired, quite enough to respond fully to all the simple questions I'd posed. But Danny had failed other quizzes before this one, because he was not reading the material. My appraisal was that Danny was attempting to substitute *personal* performance for *reading* performance. But this kind of performance was bound to interfere with the course of learning I had planned for him and for his classmates.

---

3. Especially in a summer course, I believe that brief reading-based quizzes can be a tremendous reading motivator. I never assign high stakes to these brief and easy tests, but I assign them, as I tell my students, precisely because I myself, once a highly motivated but also overburdened and often simply distracted undergraduate, used to wish that my professors would implement this one small motivating device to keep me honest when circumstances otherwise tempted me to put something on the back burner. My quizzes are pedagogical "carrots," you might say, never "sticks."
4. This reminds me of another lesson I learned on my feet; if you're drawn to quizzes as a pedagogical device, it's best to type and duplicate them ahead of class than to call out the questions "live."

I told Danny that he needed to quickly respond to as many questions as he could while I collected other students' quizzes; but I was shaky as I made my way around that classroom. I found that I was greatly off my balance, unusually uncertain about what to do. How did I respond firmly, yet fairly, to what I clearly perceived as performative jesting at my expense? How much of a stand should I make on behalf of my "dignity" (something about which, I always feel a hefty—and, I hope, healthy—measure of irony)? How much of this perverse humor could I tolerate without opening myself to the scorn of other students? How did I extend the benefit of doubt to Danny, allow for the possibility that his troubles might be exacerbated by, if not outright *evidence* of, an undisclosed learning disability or carefully covered personal problem of some other kind? How would I balance the need for something like focus—and, yes, order—in the classroom against the visible but curious underlife being displayed by this outrageous student?

Underlying all of these concerns, I felt, was one crucial consideration: Where exactly did my audience stand? What was the larger group's posture toward what seemed to me a freakish kind of classroom theater? I have observed that, in circumstances of collective outrage, groups sometimes tacitly assign a spokesperson; might a silent majority sanction Danny's claim that I was conducting this course inappropriately? Might I have selected such tepid reading material that this bizarre performance represented a more tempting focus for a summer evening? Momentarily, the confidence we profess in order to function at all abandoned me completely: the jester in this classroom seemed to be Danny, but might it not be me? Now, these might be productive ruminations during office hours alone, or on the drive to or from class; I do not wish them on anyone right in the classroom itself!

After a minute or two that felt like as many hours, I had collected all the other quizzes. Not trusting my own potential reactions, I proceeded nervously up the aisle to where Danny sat; I could see that he had not filled out a single answer on the short quiz. This did not surprise me but it did make me feel misused. The requests for repeated questions and extra time had been put to no constructive purpose. "I need your quiz," I said to Danny, hoping he could not hear the waver of self-mistrust that I heard in my own voice. At this moment, though, he saw fit to begin crying out "You're KILLING me here! You're just KILLING me!" To be quite honest, I think that my intellect abandoned me in this hellish instant and my instincts took over. Instantly, if accidentally, it dawned on me that humor was the only respectable posture with which to answer this outburst. So, with what must have been the weariest of smiles, I snatched the quiz from bellowing Danny's hand with a tennis-swing, and I turned to walk, with the batch of quizzes, back to the front of the room. My back to Danny—who was still accusing me of killing him but by now less loudly—I took a deep breath and summoned the emotional reserve we must have on hand for house-fires and the like. Over my shoulder, I called back: "And I wouldn't call this murder, Danny; I'd call it suicide."

At this moment, something illuminating—and, for me, tremendously instructive—happened in that classroom, something I had not calculated on; the whole class, Danny momentarily excluded, *roared with laughter*! What I heard was, without a doubt, the uncomplicated sound of a roomful of *friends*— well-intended people who were at once relieved that humor had diffused this encounter and eager to bring about the functioning learning environment they had signed up for—and I felt as though a painful boil had been lanced. The *group* politics declared by this laughter itself subdued Danny on that weird evening and the collective memory of it tamed Danny's underlife in our later classes, too. Remarkably, Danny began to read for class and, although his contributions were always unique, they at least began to sound grounded in what we were reading. In that instructive moment it was clear that the group—whose noncommittal silence had initially been a mysterious anxiety for me—was itself poised anxiously, waiting to witness *and take my measure by* my own eventual response to Danny's sustained disrespect. Now, and with benefit of hindsight, I am convinced that, had I found a less positive way of handling Danny's screaming—had I, for instance, given way then and there to an egoistic tantrum of my own, replete with vindications and threats—all might have gone differently.[5] In matching Danny's outburst, I would have compromised my professed commitment to respectful conduct and been drawn into a mode of behavior that I did not feel. More importantly, I would have failed to learn what has since become a central classroom tenet for me regarding resistance: Unless you yourself give way to an unseemly disregard for a student—any student, but especially a heinously disruptive student—the group is likely to be on the side of function and productivity: likely, that is, to be on *your* side.

There are moments, indeed, when extending respect can seem downright Herculean, but I now proceed with the assurance that, when respect is your bottom line, you can generally count on receiving it in turn, even in dicey classroom situations. In a strategy that was accidental but effective, I opted to go along with Danny's vaudeville, but I turned the joke back to the way classroom authority functioned. You might say that Danny forced me to terminate the honeymoon we implicitly prolong in the classroom when we pretend not to inhabit—in fact, work to displace—the authority we represent as teachers. His resistance—rightly enough—was aimed not at Rutgers University or at the social order, but against the authority vested in *me,* the woman who was asking him to read two nights a week during the summer; I guess I opted to be sincere instead of diverting that resistance against some anonymous authority as though I myself stood apart from it. In this bizarre moment, I allowed Danny's theatrically cast slaughter to prevail as a description of our institutional and interpersonal relationship. "You're killing me" is not an altogether delusional description, after all, of the way a student who

---

5. This is certainly not to say, however, that a teacher should never remind a belligerent student of campus policies about behavior like Danny's. My sense was that Danny did not require outside intervention at that stage, and this proved to be a correct appraisal.

has not done the course work—and not taken responsibility for that—stands in regard to his teacher. Its hyperbole, of course, but denying such hyperbole would itself have been craziness. I only adjusted *the agent* implied in his narrative from me to him—from murder to suicide—and the group paid me an important tribute, I now think, for that momentary and instinctive willingness to blink. Recapping Robert Pattison, Miriam T. Chaplin (1991) formulates a statement that glosses my long-ago experience in the classroom with Danny perfectly. "Literacy," she contends, "is not merely communication. Literacy is also behavior that exhibits a consciousness of the problems and uses of language and the ability to express this consciousness in ways evolved and sanctioned by the group" (p. 95). You might say the class taught Danny that evening; he and I, conversely, may have learned something important.

In the honors writing class that followed my more recent student's belligerent email, you can bet I scanned the room and scrutinized its sender: He is as quirky and blunt in spoken conversation with his classmates as the email would have foreshadowed, and many of his cohorts seem to treat his social awkwardness with well-worn irony but also with a warm kind of callousness. He writes far better than many students who declare a hatred of English classes, and I can see why he is an honors student. He is youthful and naive (despite a posture of world-weariness), and also smart (despite an I-couldn't-care-less body language); understandably, he is impatient with what he perceives as gates and gatekeepers: his brashness says all of that. So he would prefer to be somewhere other than in my course three days a week at noon; in the big picture, is this such a transgression? We've been discussing essays on privacy and public space and soon he raises his hand, his expression grumpy: Someone among us is going to hear about an error or contradiction in our thinking, and probably not in a tactfully formulated manner, either. These things, too, he is learning. But I can't suppress a smile as I point toward him; I'm somehow grateful for the disagreement, and, after all, I know—I recall—resistance can assume more trying shapes than this.

Works Cited

Anderson, Worth, Cynthia Best, Alycia Black, John Hurst, Brandt Miller, and Susan Miller. 1990. "Cross-Curricular Underlife: A Collaborative Report on Ways with Academic Words." *College Composition and Communication* 41.1: 11–36.

Brooke, Robert. 1987. "Underlife and Writing Instruction." *College Composition and Communication* 38.2: 141–53.

Chaplin, Miriam T. 1991. "Teaching for Literacy in Socio-Cultural and Political Contexts." In *Composition and Resistance* edited by C. Mark Hurlbert and Michael Blitz, 95–104. Portsmouth: Boynton/Cook.

Goffman, Erving. 1961. *Asylums: Essays on the Social Situation of Mental Patients and Other Inmates.* New York: Anchor.

——— 1963. *Stigma: Notes on the Management of Spoiled Identity.* Englewood Cliffs, NJ: Prentice-Hall.

6

"Is It My Problem if They Can't Keep up with Me?"

Ball Hogs, Point Guards, and Student Participation in the Composition Classroom

John Regan

One week into the fall 1993 semester at the University of Rhode Island, I was reading a colleague's evaluation of one of my classes from the previous semester. The reviewer's comments were complimentary, so naturally I thought they were insightful, until I reached the following sentence: "Perhaps John works too hard at coming across as knowledgeable and well-prepared." This comment puzzled me. What's wrong with appearing competent and prepared? I just didn't get it.

During that semester, an experience with one of my classes helped me get it. After my morning section of first-year composition, Nathan, a student in the class, approached. He wanted to talk more about the assigned reading, excerpts from Studs Terkel's (1974) *Working*. Nathan was an energetic student who seemed older than most of the other students (he later told me he was twenty-three) and who didn't interact with them before or after class. During our first group discussion he raised several perceptive points about the relationship between the lives of the *Working* people and larger economic structures, displaying intellectual acuity and some understanding of Marx and Adam Smith. I was delighted to have such an engaged, informed student.

It's fascinating how what we perceive as positive classroom situations can quickly sour. Nathan, my outstanding student, continued to stand out, but I soon realized his exuberance was becoming a problem. In our next few class discussions, I noticed that some students grimaced and rolled their eyes when Nathan spoke while others looked away. Always the first to respond to every discussion question, Nathan didn't seem too interested in what his classmates had to say; when they spoke, which was becoming less and less frequent, he thumbed through his book in search of his next point. Nathan conveyed the attitude that what any other student had to say distracted from the true business at hand—his own dialogue with the teacher.

At first I used simple "teacher tricks" to rectify what I thought was a minor problem. For example, I pretended not to see his raised hand or I would acknowledge it and say, "Let's hear from somebody else." But Nathan's aggressive charges through my subtle barriers combined with the rest of the class' reticence to seize openings and speak up proved a fatal combination, and our class discussions went nowhere. The other students seemed to have turned on Nathan, and my enthusiastic responses to his input in the first few class discussions not only validated his behavior in his own eyes, but also alienated the rest of the class; they had clearly turned on him, and, by extension, tuned me out.

I began to think about Nathan's aggressive conversational style and desire to monopolize every discussion in the context of Deborah Tannen's (1991) and Carol Gilligan's (1993) work on gender, language, and communication. As a domineering male in a predominately female classroom, Nathan seemed to view classroom conversations as contests: According to Gilligan (1993), female students generally try to move classroom discussions toward consensus and embrace compromise, whereas male students battle to see who is right and who is wrong (Jarratt, 1991, p. 111). In composition studies, the most "argumentative" male students are most often represented as emblematic of a win-at-all-costs culture, and the composition teacher handles the problem by creating a nurturing classroom environment that will serve as a corrective. However, some in composition and rhetoric question whether composition pedagogies based on conflict avoidance are equipped to handle such students. For example, in "Feminism and Composition: The Case for Conflict," Susan Jarratt (1991) cautions that composition pedagogies that seek to avoid conflict may in fact reify dangerous practices. As she observes, "Advising a female to 'swallow' without reply a conventional male reaction to a woman's experience has serious consequences" (p. 111). Yet others caution against the demonizing of male students and call for a closer analysis of the social and psychological concerns of adolescent males as a way to better understand and teach young men (Connors, 1996; Tobin, 1996). In his analysis of male students in the first-year writing class, Lad Tobin (1996) argues that composition instructors are too quickly dismissive of "resisting" male students because most teachers have a poor understanding of adolescent male culture. If teachers can gain a deeper understanding of adolescent male culture, Tobin suggests, they will be more adept at dealing with the male student's disruptive behavior and challenges to their authority.

However, Nathan differed from the type of student that Tobin describes because he in no way sought to challenge or undermine my authority; in fact, part of his problem was an overwhelmingly heightened sense of the value of my authority. And while the style of Nathan's reaction may have been conventionally male, his ideas were not—he often argued passionately for an open-minded consideration of feminist ideas. Unlike Tobin's more familiar student type, the obnoxious, cap-wearing, white middle-class young man who loudly espouses misogynistic views and even more loudly denounces the ideas of any feminist writer—or any writer suspected of harboring feminist sympathies—regardless of whether or not (and it's usually not) he's read the text, Nathan was especially difficult precisely because he was so insightful. Students resisted his ideas not on merit, but because they didn't want to encourage him. For example, in one class Nathan considered the political implications of an Adrienne Rich (2002) poem, but the students resisted this way of looking at the work, and I knew we were at a stand-off. He had opened up a compelling line of inquiry worth pursuing on an intellectual level, but I instantly recognized that to follow it would be to validate his domineering attitude. Luckily, class time expired; saved by the bell, I desperately stumbled back to my corner office.

If Nathan were on a basketball court rather than in a classroom, we would call him a "ball hog." Ball hogs are overzealous players who are always first to shoot and the last to pass; they are primarily interested in their own shots, which leads the rest of the team to stop moving and grind to a halt. Certainly my class was grinding to a halt, and what made matters worse was Nathan's intellectual ability. Often, "ball hogs" have a higher regard for their own intellectual acuity than seems warranted, yet they are most dangerous when they are good scorers.

Because the vast majority of student behavioral problems are better addressed by individual conferencing rather than in-class confrontation, I scheduled a conference with Nathan. During our meeting, I recited the benefits of collaboration and teamwork in the classroom. I thought I was compelling and convincing; however, Nathan looked puzzled.

"I just don't get it," he said.

"I appreciate the level of your participation, but I was wondering if we could try to get other students involved."

"At the beginning of the course you said to come to class prepared and ready to work, and that's what I've done. Now it seems as if you're telling me not to."

"No, not at all. Just let other people get involved; aren't you interested in what they have to say?"

"I don't think most of them are even doing the reading. Is it my problem if they can't keep up with me?"

I mumbled something about how that wasn't the issue and how I was certain that the other students had much of value to say, but for a moment I feared that he might have a point. In comparison to my other sections, this one did seem especially disengaged, even for so early in the semester. As I sat down to read the first set of drafts, I thought about the disappointment that I've heard many teachers describe when even lively discussions yield lethargic papers, but when I finished reading the drafts, the students' ideas and insights impressed me. Most had considered sophisticated angles to the material. Without Nathan's looming presence to contend with, the students explored original ideas and forged quality work. During a conference with Karen, an insightful student who had produced an especially thoughtful paper, I asked her why she didn't mention any of her ideas in class. She replied, "I don't know" in a vacant voice that suggested that she really meant to say, "I do know, but I don't want to get into it." Because our class would soon be doing more collaborative activities, certainly Nathan would recognize their intellectual abilities and appreciate his peers.

Yet while activities such as small group discussion and peer review isolated the problem, the problem still festered. The groups without Nathan functioned extremely well, reading each other's drafts attentively and writing furiously in response to my peer review questions. On the other hand, the shift to group work seemed to catch Nathan off guard. In small group discussions he often raised his hand to get my attention, as if he needed someone to verify the value of his remarks, to acknowledge that he had put more points on the scoreboard. While I constantly admonished him to "Talk about that with your group," Nathan's group seemed to work around him. Even though his peer reviewers worked assiduously to provide feedback on his drafts, he distrusted their responses, and repeatedly asked me after class what I thought about his work. When I refused to look at it and told him that at this stage he should consider the peer responses, he looked heartbroken. Nathan's response could be interpreted as a typical male student's resistance to collaborative work. In "Teaching and Learning as a Man," Robert Connors (1996) suggests that many male students are uncomfortable with what they perceive as the diffuse nature of collaborative work. Connors observes, "I have noticed that young men want clearly defined individual credit for the work they do and the roles they play in groups" (p. 154). Yet, while his observation may accurately describe Nathan in this respect, his recommendation that given this resistance we may have to teach men differently than women is suspect. Teamwork and cooperation are invaluable skills and, regardless of gender, if someone needs to improve in those areas, they should be given more collaborative assignments, not fewer. It's always easier to teach people things that they already know how to do well.

Clearly Nathan's conceptions of outstanding classroom performance and the student–teacher relationship were inextricably bound with his view of himself as a successful student, but I was surprised at how firmly entrenched those conceptions were.

Certainly he was playing out a familiar role, but he seemed bright enough to be more flexible. In "Reconstructing Authority: Negotiating Power in Democratic Learning Sites," Candace Spigelman (2001) offers some valuable insight into how successful students view themselves and underscores the difficulty of getting students to reconceive of their roles in the classroom. Using sophomore students as peer group leaders in her first-year writing course, she was surprised that within their groups they often struggled to make independent decisions—to exercise their authority—because they seemed overly concerned with doing "exactly" what she, the teacher, wanted them to do. She traces their resistance to assuming positions of authority to their traditional notions of their own roles in the classroom:

> In retrospect, I realize that [their] discomfort . . . was related to their reluctance to assume teacherly authority, and that this reluctance was not simply a matter of their personal choice but a function of the powerful social and institutional forces that constructed them as "good college students." . . . As Rick Evans explains, citing [Kenneth] Bruffee, many successful students "typically assume that the only important classroom relationship is that 'one-to-one' relationship between themselves as individual (and isolated) students and their teacher." (p. 42)

Spigelman reports that while her group leaders seemed to have warmly embraced their readings in composition pedagogy, their practice often didn't reflect such an appreciation; in a similar way, Nathan conveyed an open-mindedness about our course readings that belied his domineering attitude. For instance, when we discussed Paulo Freire's (2002) "The Banking Concept of Education," Nathan unleashed a forceful monolog that lambasted the banker–teacher's lecture-based pedagogy. I know that I let his lecture on the inadequacies of lecturing go on for too long; when I finally cut him off, Karen smiled, and I suspect that many other students picked up on the irony.

My inability to persuade Nathan led me to consider how important it is to articulate what we consider outstanding classroom behavior in terms that our students can understand. In the classroom as a "contact zone"—Mary Louis Pratt's (2002) term for a "social spac[e] where cultures meet, clash, and grapple with each other" (p. 607)—we often reach an impasse between the students' language and our own: metaphors that are satisfactory to us are often incomprehensible to them. In Nathan's case, something had to give: How could I transform his ball hog mentality into that of a point guard? During my second conference with Nathan, I decided to play on his interest in basketball, which he revealed in a journal entry. We talked about basketball in general and then I explained the difference between ball hogs and point guards: Whereas ball hogs are interested only in shooting and scoring, point guards do everything. Point guards are responsible for how the team functions; they help others and get their own points as well. The truly great basketball players, I explained, have point guard mentalities when they're on the court; they make those around them as well as themselves better, and the very best students do the same thing when they're in the classroom.

"Nathan," I said, " I'd like you to start thinking more like a point guard, and I wonder if you can do it. They often call the point guard 'the coach on the floor,' and I'm curious to see if you have the ability to do this in the classroom. I consider this the highest level of student achievement."

The idea of "added responsibility" appealed to Nathan, and he seemed eager to try out his new role. While I was concerned that he might become even more overbearing, his transformation was, in fact, abrupt and somewhat amusing. In our next class, many students looked puzzled when he restrained himself during our discussion; they were even more startled when he expressed interest in what they were saying. The students knew something had happened, and they couldn't quite figure out what, but after a while they didn't care; they were too interested in expressing their own ideas. I was stunned by how quickly the class dynamic changed, and students who once had sat silently now freely participated.

Perhaps what ultimately persuaded Nathan to alter his behavior was not any sense of the collective good, but a desire to achieve a higher level of individual performance. The point guard metaphor presented terms that he understood; he knew that in basketball terms what separates the star from the superstar, the Dominique Wilkins from the Michael Jordan, is the ability to think more like a point guard than a ball hog and thus make the other players around you better. And these terms helped me to reconsider my role in the classroom and my colleague's comments about my teaching. Was I a "ball hog" teacher? Was I, as my colleague had suggested, perhaps a bit too focused on what I said and how I acted in the classroom and, by implication, a bit less concerned about what my students said and did? Certainly, my enthusiastic validation of Nathan during the first few classes revealed something about me to my students, yet I think it went further than that—my responses to what they said too often became the last word, as if I were intent on saying something profound rather than helping them to say something profound. Sometimes I still impulsively hog the ball or grab it away from a student—as Warren Zevon (1978) sang, "I'm just an excitable boy"—but I'm getting better at working within the team structure.

And as further evidence that I don't always have to hog the ball, I'll resist the obligatory "Look what a great teacher I am now" ending of many teacher stories. In a review of two books of teacher narratives, Kate Ronald (1992) observes, "It's difficult not to become the hero of your own teaching story. It's almost impossible not to search for a happy ending to a teaching story" (p. 256). While my story does have a happy ending, I certainly don't look at myself as a hero, nor is Nathan one; he caused a problem and I exacerbated it. If there are heroes, it's the other students in the class, who responded to an awkward situation with verve and maturity. They could have looked upon the situation as an excuse to slack off—and I have no doubt that other classes that I have had would have done just that. When the opportunity to participate finally came, they seized it. As one student wrote in her final journal entry, "This is the first class that I really felt like what I said mattered. Thank you."

Throughout the next few years I frequently saw Nathan around campus; he never seemed to have a shortage of friends. Once when we passed in the hallway, he said,

"Hi, coach . . . I don't know why I called you 'coach.' "

"It happens," I replied.

Works Cited

Connors, Robert J. 1996. "Teaching and Learning as a Man." *College English* 58: 137–57.

Freire, Paulo. 2002. "The Banking Concept of Education." In *Ways of Reading: An Anthology for Writers,* 6th ed., edited by David Bartholomae and Anthony Petrosky, 259–275. Boston: Bedford/St. Martins.

Gilligan, Carol. 1993. In *a Different Voice: Psychological Theory and Women's Development.* Cambridge, MA: Harvard UP.

Jarratt, Susan C. 1991. "Feminism and Composition: The Case for Conflict." In *Contending with Words,* edited by Patricia Harkin and John Schlib. New York: MLA.

Pratt, Mary Louise. 2002. "Arts of the Contact Zone." In *Ways of Reading: An Anthology for Writers,* 6th edition, edited by David Bartholomae and Anthony Petrosky, 605–18. Boston: Bedford.

Rich, Adrienne. 2002. "When We Dead Amwaken: Writing as Re-Vision." In *Ways of Reading: An Anthology for Writers,* 6th ed., edited by David Bartholomae and Anthony Petrosky, 627–640. Boston: Bedford/St. Martins.

Ronald, Kate. 1999. "How to Tell a True Teaching Story." *College English* 62: 255–64.

Spigelman, Candace. 2001. "Reconstructing Authority: Negotiating Power in Democratic Learning Sites." *Composition Studies* 29(1): 27–50.

Tannen, Deborah. 1991. *You Just Don't Understand Me: Men and Women in Conversation.* New York: Ballantine.

Terkel, Studs. 1974. *Working: People Talk About What They Do All Day and How They Feel About What They Do.* New York: Pantheon.

Tobin, Lad. 1996. "Car Wrecks, Baseball Caps, and Man-to-Man Defense: The Personal Narratives of Adolescent Males." *College English* 58: 158–75.

Zevon, Warren. 1978. "Excitable Boy." On *Excitable Boy* [CD]. New York: Asylum Records.

7

White Indian Up Front

Building Learning Communities in the
"Postcolonial"/Indigenized Classroom

Paul W. DePasquale

A few years ago, shortly before the Christmas midsession exam in my English 101, one of my students, "Rhonda," came to the office. She was visibly worried, upset, and didn't know what to do about her "problem," as she called it. I invited her to have a seat and explain what the matter was. "My husband just shot a moose," she said. The expression on Rhonda's face told me that this was something of a mixed blessing. "I don't want to go home right now, but I have to." Home was about 300 miles north of Edmonton, Alberta, in a remote Cree community. "My family needs me to help clean it. I have to go." When my student asked if she could write the midsession after the holidays, I wasn't sure how to respond; while Rhonda clearly wasn't requesting a two-week extension on a term paper because she wanted to go to Cancun, Mexico, with friends, an excuse I had heard recently from a student in another class, I wasn't quite sure that needing to go home to clean a moose was reasonable grounds to reschedule an exam. Buying myself some time to consider her request, I asked if there wasn't someone else in the family who could do the job for her. "I'm the only one who knows how to do this," she replied. "My *Cheechum* [grandmother] taught me when I was a little girl, and I'll teach my kids as soon as they can hold a knife steady. My husband can help a bit, but he's pretty squeamish."

After further conversation about her situation, I realized that going home to clean the moose was only a small part of why my student felt that she needed to return home: Rhonda had left four small children behind with her husband in order to pursue a university education. While her family was supportive of her dreams and goals at first, they were now missing her a great deal and wanting her to come home as soon as possible. Her family, she said, wasn't making out too well without her. In the end, I agreed to let Rhonda write the midsession in January, although I was concerned that, because of family circumstances and pressure, she might not return to university after the holidays. My student had shown much promise in the course to date, had done well on her midterm and first two essays, and I didn't want to see her slip through the cracks, as I had several other students in a similar situation.

Experiences like this one with Rhonda have been fairly common during my ten years of teaching composition and literature courses to Aboriginal and non-Aboriginal students.[1] At the time, I was a sessional English instructor in the Transition Year Program (TYP) for Native students at the University of Alberta, a fairly large university of about 30,000 students located in Edmonton, Alberta. Today, I am an Assistant Professor of English at the University of Winnipeg, a small undergraduate institution of about 6,000 students in Winnipeg, Manitoba. Teaching First Nations students has been an intensely challenging and sometimes difficult experience. (It has also been highly rewarding, although this isn't my focus here.) Very little in either my academic or pedagogical training has prepared me to interact in a helpful and effective way with students who face a range of emotional and socioeconomic barriers to their education. And I'm not sure if my own mixed racial identity—I am a Status Indian but look more Caucasian than Indian because I am also parts Welsh and Ukrainian—makes teaching Natives any more or less difficult. In any case, my teaching experiences have raised many anxieties and have forced me to think not only about what, how, and why I teach, but also about my pedagogical role and utility in the classroom. While I haven't found any sure-fire solutions to the challenges I've encountered, this essay shares some of my successful—and not so successful—strategies in teaching First Nations audiences. I hope it will encourage others to think more about their own pedagogical assumptions in relation to students from groups that have traditionally been underrepresented in our postsecondary educational systems.

My first TYP English 101 class is not a time that I think back on proudly. I remember feeling kind of nervous about standing at the front of the classroom for the first time as an instructor, and my effort to hide my nervousness probably made me seem a bit more stiff and formal than I usually am. I opened the class by handing out and discussing the course outline in a way that probably seemed too brisk and authoritative. So that students could get to know me a little, I talked

---

1. The terminology used to describe Canada's Indigenous peoples, such as "Aboriginal," "Native," "Indian," "First Nations," and "First Peoples," can be highly problematic, as Greg Young-Ing explains in "Talking Terminology: What's in a Word and What's Not," in "First Voices, First Words." Ed. Thomas King. *Prairie Fire*. Special Issue. 22.3 (2001): 130–40. For the sake of variety, I refer to Native peoples in Canada as "First Nations," "Aboriginals," "Natives," and, in certain contexts, because my own family still uses the term to describe ourselves even though it is considered derogatory by many, "Indians." Interestingly, the definition of "Native American," the preferred term to describe Indigenous peoples of the United States, seems to be broadening to include the Aboriginal peoples of Canada. Note, for example, the Smithsonian Institute's recent decision to include three Canadian Native communities—the Métis in St. Laurent, Manitoba; the Inuit in Nunavut; and Kanawake First Nation in Quebec—in its National Museum for Native Americans, scheduled to open in 2004.

about my various academic achievements and accomplishments. I told the class that I had completed my Honors BA in English at the University of Waterloo, and my MA in Creative Writing at the University of Alberta, where I was currently enrolled in the PhD program, preparing to write a dissertation on representations of Native North Americans in early–modern colonial writings. As though these details would somehow impress students and underscore my authority in this particular classroom, I discussed some of the ways that my approach to colonial discourses had been informed by scholars such as Homi Bhabha, Peter Hulme, Mary B. Campbell, and others, and then explained that my emphasis on Aboriginal agency in Anglo-American encounters was an important departure from the emphasis on English mastery in the writings of Stephen Greenblatt, Jeffrey Knapp, and others. This theoretical overview was followed by a quick highlight of my scholarships and awards, after which I gave a little speech on matters relating to university policies on plagiarism, cheating, and other academic offences. Finally, because I was hoping to make a good impression on the first day of class, I decided not to take up the full seventy-five minutes talking and, instead, to let students out a few minutes early. Thinking back to my rather unfriendly, distant approach to students that first day, I remember some pretty scared, intimidated, and put-off looking faces as they packed their things and headed for the door.

Today, of course, I realize that such an impersonal, officious beginning does little to help students feel comfortable on the first day of class or to suggest that our classroom will be a welcoming and vibrant learning community over the course of the year. Creating a sense of community in the classroom is important, in part to help students overcome feelings of isolation, as educators such as Alexander Astin (1985, p. 165), and Nancy Shapiro and Jodi Levine (1999, pp. 3–4) have recognized. In my experience, the need for a sense of community is particularly strong among First Nations students, many of whom find the university an intimidating, even frightening place. Most of the Aboriginal students I have taught are the first in their families to attend university, and many arrive here filled with negative images of educational institutions and feeling highly doubtful about their chances of success. These images and expectations have been shaped in large part by Canada's colonial and neocolonial history of assimilationist strategies, such as the Residential School experience, where children were removed from their families, forced to stop speaking their languages and practicing their traditions, and made to conform to "civilized" Western ways. Indeed, the negative perception toward formal education among family and friends back home is one of the obstacles that many Aboriginals continue to face throughout their time at university.

Further, students who are far away from home, often for the first time, frequently experience a sense of alienation and cultural displacement when they arrive in a foreign and intimidatingly large urban environment, such as Edmonton, with a population of about one million, or Winnipeg, with about 700,000 people. While students I have taught from other cultural backgrounds sometimes experience similar emotions and dislocations, Aboriginal students have an unusually high degree of difficulty adjusting to university life. (Retention is a huge challenge: even with support programs and services in place, the dropout rate for those in their first year ranges from about twenty-five to thirty percent in my experience). With such challenges in mind, I feel that one of the instructor's most important roles is to help students learn that the university is a comfortable place that they can eventually learn to negotiate and perhaps even enjoy.

The first day of class and the tone that the professor sets can have an impact on how well things go from here, both for individual students and the class as a whole. Now on the first day, I try to set aside many of the ideas I have learned about maintaining a professional distance from students, ideas I seem to have absorbed during many years as a student observing professors. This has meant trying to undo years of conscious and unconscious learning in a Western educational context that prizes things like self-control, discipline, structure, and hierarchy, things that my scholarly work has taught me are fundamentally imperialist in outlook, in the way that they seek to assert authority, privilege, and power. In this process of undoing, I have tried to learn and relearn from family members and other First Nations people. For example, if you listen to Aboriginals talk to other people for the first time, you may notice that they often begin by locating themselves within a particular geographic and familial context. Aboriginal peoples, not unlike others, are very interested to learn about a person's family ties and connectedness to a community. Today, I am in the practice of introducing myself to students on a more personal level, even before I begin talking about the course's content or requirements. I tell students that I was raised in Brantford, Ontario, just outside the Six Nations Reserve, where my Mohawk father and his family are from. I add that my mother's parents were Welsh and Ukrainian, and that, while I spent much time on the reserve as a kid, I grew up in the city, in a fairly white, middle-class environment. I tell them that, for reasons that could probably take up a book, there was a lot of shame and embarrassment in my family so that, as a kid, I never knew about my Indian ancestry, or even, more strangely, that I was actually related by blood to those people I called my aunts, uncles, and cousins out on the reserve. Of course, I had my suspicions, but the point is that my family never discussed these things in an open way. It was not until about 1985, the year that the Canadian government introduced Bill C-31, which made it possible for my family to apply for reinstatement of the Indian Status we lost when my Mohawk grandmother left the reserve, with my father who was a young boy, and married a non-Native, that my father began to speak openly about his Aboriginal background. Only then did the fact of our Indianness become something that was okay to talk about. Today, my family is proud of our Mohawk ancestry, and we return to the Six Nations to learn more about our Iroquois community's rich past and strong present.

A more personal self introduction can be effective whether or not a teacher is able to "identify," culturally, with students. At a recent workshop on "Teaching Canadian First Nations Writing" at the University of Alberta, Renate Eigenbrod, a scholar of German descent who teaches at Lakehead University in Thunder Bay and who has taught for over a decade at reserves in Northern Ontario, said that she regularly opens her courses by talking about her German background. She even introduces Emma Lee Warrior's (1998) "Compatriots," a short story about a rather naive German woman who visits a First Nations community to learn about Indians in a way that will satisfy her idealized, romanticized curiosity, as a way of addressing her own otherness. Aboriginal peoples, Eigenbrod observes, are fascinated to learn about other peoples and places, and are appreciative of their instructor's willingness to engage them on a personal level. I have seen a similar interest and appreciation in my own classes, and have found that the introduction can be a useful way of establishing what Sharon Baiocco and Jamie DeWaters (1998), in their discussion of " 'Supertraits' of Excellent Teachers," term "expressiveness" (which includes sociability and friendliness) and "empathy" (which suggests that the professor will be a good listener and will value student ideas) (p. 111). Students appreciate that I speak to them, not as a peer, but as a person who brings a particular context to the literatures that I read and interpret.

As a teacher of Aboriginal literatures by such authors as Louis Bird, Eden Robinson, Louise Erdrich, Thomas King, Lee Maracle, Jeannette Armstrong, Paula Gunn Allen, Harry Robinson, and others, I have seen the ways that Aboriginal idioms, colloquialisms, and modes of expression are "indigenizing" the English language.[2] Increasingly, because of the influence of my own First Nations background and teaching experiences, I am recognizing the value of seeing and theorizing my classroom as another indigenized space, particularly because I teach in a field where, according to John Docker (1995) in "The Neocolonial Assumption in University Teaching of English," there still exists "a ruling anglocentric assumption . . . [in which] the white colonising society removes the indigenous culture to an inferior level by virtue of the superiority of the metropolitan culture it is establishing" (p. 443). By engaging students on a more personal level, rather than on the level of a guarded professionalism, the professor has the potential to disrupt the traditional teacher–student relationship that is modeled on what Franz Fanon calls a "hierarchy of cultures" (qtd. in Docker, 1995, p. 443). Students seem to appreciate my openness, and many can relate to someone who is himself engaged in a complex and sometimes uncomfortable process of working out difficult questions about race and identity. My self-introduction thus raises questions and issues that we will explore over the year, in our discussions of a range of literary texts that address the problematics of race, ethnicity, and identity, from texts like Margaret Laurence's (1998) "The Loons," Bharati Mukherjee's

2. For a discussion of the development and politics of "Aboriginal patois," including "Red English" and "Rez English," see Greg Young-Ing, "Aboriginal Text in Context," in Ruffo, (2001).

(1998) "The Tenant," Alice Walker's (1998) "Everyday Use," Amy Tan's (1998) "Two Kinds," and Austin Clarke's (1998) "The Motor Car," to Maria Campbell's (1973) *Halfbreed* and Louise Erdrich's (1993) *Love Medicine*. It demonstrates the connectedness of literary texts to our own lives, our own senses of identity and self, and highlights in important ways the usefulness and applicability of the texts we read and interpret. Further, by sharing with students a bit of their personal, as well as professional selves, teachers promote openness and reciprocity. One of the benefits is that those who might not ordinarily speak up in class are encouraged to see that the classroom is a safe and comfortable space in which to articulate their views, and these students are often motivated to put in the extra effort required to improve their written communication skills.

One of my frustrations in teaching First Nations students is in trying to evaluate students, many of whom are reserve-educated and arrive at university vastly unprepared for a formal Western education. It is not often in my experience that the English language skills of the average first-year Aboriginal student match those of the average mainstream freshman. Obviously, this detail points not to a lack of cognitive or linguistic abilities on the part of Natives, but to a lack of educational resources on reserves, and, even more importantly, to a fundamental difference between Indigenous and Western modes of perceiving and learning. Recognizing this discrepancy does not make the instructor's task any easier. Even before I first read educational philosopher Arthur E. Lean's classic 1968 essay, "The Farce Called 'Grading' " many years ago, I felt ambivalent about the grading process and about competitive models for evaluating students. My uncertainty is compounded in relation to First Nations students, whose values and experiences do not readily conform to competitive, hierarchical ways of measuring an individual's learning, development, and "progress." This incompatibility was recently foregrounded here in Winnipeg when a group of Native Studies students at the University of Manitoba had their grades for a half-credit, off-campus course on Aboriginal healing methods reduced by the Dean of Arts and the Chair of Native Studies. The instructor of the course, elder Jules Lavallee, awarded marks in the high nineties to nearly twenty students who attended his course at the Red Willow Lodge. "Because of the nature of the course, a lot of self-discovery happens," the elder said, explaining the high grades. "A lot of it is personal application. There is content, but a lot of it is process." The university's administration, however, considered such high marks unacceptable, and reduced students' grades by about a full letter grade. Lavallee, like others, feels that a pass/fail system would better serve students taking certain kinds of courses, but the University of Manitoba insists on a mark that can be worked into a grade point average ("Cultural Clash," n.p.).

On the subject of grading, other anxieties arise: What kinds of assignments should I give to my students, and what criteria should I follow when evaluating them? Is it fair to expect that persons whose first language is Omushkego or Anishnaabe, say, and not English, and who come from cultures that value the spoken word over the written, can demonstrate, by the end of a first-year English class, the ability to write a sophisticated academic paper that is free from technical and stylistic errors? If we expect mainstream students to have developed such an ability by year end, as many professors do, shouldn't we expect the same proficiencies of First Nations and other "minority" students? Shouldn't we be raising the bar for all instead of lowering it for some?

But would placing less emphasis on the traditional academic essay, or the final exam for that matter, really represent a lowering of the bar? Couldn't we search for alternative ways of assessing students who come from cultures unlike our own? We might, for example, develop curriculum that would enable students to respond to literary and other cultural texts through more artistic rather than academic means, such as creative writing, music, painting, and sculpture. But an obvious difficulty arises: How could an instructor trained in English assess, with integrity, an object like a soapstone carving or a medicine song modeled after a traditional Inuit chant? How would my Departmental Review Committee, which processes student appeals, assess a student's protest that her Haida-inspired artwork received only a C? Such a course could be cotaught with an instructor from another department, but would this guarantee that the necessary skills and criteria would be in place to evaluate students' performance fairly? And on the subject of final exams, I decided last year to experiment by replacing my usual final exam format, which asks the traditional passage identification, definition, and essay type of questions, with a take-home exam with a creative option. The experiment proved a disaster for many; rather than, as I had hoped, being inspired and motivated by an unconventional exam that offered room to explore their own interests, many students' attendance, motivation, and performance dropped off, in fact, soon after the Christmas exam, which tested them on the traditional kinds of questions. Several did not complete the required readings, class participation waned, and many of the learning objectives that students and I had established together at the beginning of the course went unrealized. Several students even complained in their course evaluations that they were disappointed not to have a traditional final exam as they felt that this would have given them a more structured and disciplined learning experience. In any case, while I have serious doubts about the long-term value for students of a traditional exam format, I continue to use it as an encouragement to them to attend class regularly and to read the assigned materials.

Evaluating students makes me especially uncomfortable when I have to assess students who have not had the "opportunity" of receiving a Western secondary-school education that would put them on par with other undergraduates. In our current educational system in North America, one that measures students primarily on the basis of exam scores and GPAs, I am recognizing the need to evaluate First Nations students somewhat differently than I assess my more mainstream students. At the University of Alberta, for example, if I had evaluated my TYP students according to the same criteria by which I graded students in English 199, a technical communications course for Engineering students which I also taught, the failure and dropout rates for Aboriginals would have been much higher than they already were. My Engineering students, who tended to be well-educated, motivated, and highly competitive young white males, generally did not face the same socioeconomic barriers that First Nations students face. About two-thirds of my First Nations students are single mothers, for instance. Class and gender politics play definite roles in keeping these students from devoting sufficient time to their studies. Having few funds for "frills" like daycare and babysitting, and not always having family or friends nearby for support, students' attention to things like attendance and deadlines tends, for good reason, to be low on their list of priorities. Deductions for late assignments and poor attendance would, in my view, unfairly penalize and thereby discourage peoples who are already struggling to stay in school. But because the effort required to play catch up is often much more than some students are able to give, the issues surrounding the problem of how to keep them in university go way beyond simply being a supportive and encouraging instructor. At the same time, I recognize the need to achieve some balance here, to be a caring instructor who also motivates students to excel in their studies, because the professor who accepts anything less than academic rigor and excellence is clearly not preparing his or her students to meet the demands of other undergraduate courses, graduate school, or a competitive workplace after graduation. I had a conversation about this recently with a friend who works in the corporate world, who encouraged me, for the "good" of my students, she said, to adopt a "sink or swim" approach to their evaluation. I argued that, because numerous forces have put, and continue to put, many Aboriginal peoples into a disadvantaged position where they often do not possess the tools that would enable them fully to achieve a sense of economic and political independence, some measure of clemency is warranted on the part of educators so that this present generation can continue to keep the ball rolling for future generations. But the question of just how much leniency is a good thing for individual students is a very difficult one to work out in practice, however.

Another challenge is the heterogeneity of my First Nations students. When I first began teaching, I was under the kinds of naive assumptions about people from postcolonial[3] nations that Gayatri Chakravorty Spivak (1993) warns us about in *Outside in the Teaching Machine*. I assumed that all of my Aboriginal students would be interested in learning about Native literatures and cultures. I've since come to understand just how diverse the members of

---

3. The term "postcolonial" (with or without the hyphen) is also problematic. Thomas King argues that, because it tends to divide Canada's history into a tripartite scheme of precolonial, colonial, and postcolonial, the term privileges the colonial experience and denies Native peoples a history of their own outside of the arrival of Europeans in North America (see King, 1990). Anita Heiss's recent denunciation of the term in the context of Australian Aboriginal literatures is one that many indigenous authors throughout the world would agree with. Heiss observes, "[M]ost writers do not even consider the term [post-colonial] in relation to their writing at all . . . [T]he term 'post-colonialism' is meaningless to Aboriginal people, bearing in mind the political, social and economic status we currently occupy" (in Ruffo, 2001, p. 226). I find "postcolonial" a more forward-looking term than

my class can be: some are born on a reserve, while others are from a city; some are traditionalists and others nontraditionalists; some are full-blooded while others are mixed. And Canada's Aboriginal peoples fall under several distinct categories—Métis, Status, non-Status, Inuit—any of which can be further divided into numerous tribal and intertribal designations and polities. In fact, Canada's Aboriginal peoples exist today in some 608 bands in about 2,600 reserve communities, as well as in numerous urban environments. First Nations people are a complexly heterogeneous bunch, and the degrees to which we will be interested in Aboriginal literatures and issues varies enormously. I remember being quite surprised a few years ago when "Denise," a reserve-born Cree woman, asked if she could write an essay on William Carlos Williams' (1998) "The Red Wheelbarrow" rather than on a topic I had suggested, on a poem by an Aboriginal author. After listening to her clear thoughts on, and obvious enthusiasm for, Williams' poem, I welcomed her to write the essay. But I was still astonished. My reaction later made me reflect on my pedagogical assumptions: why was it so surprising that she would choose to write on a non-Native text? Now, while I still try to tailor my classes to an Aboriginal audience, choosing texts I think will appeal and matter to them, I remind myself to check in with my ideas about who the members of this audience are, and to revise these ideas wherever it seems necessary.

Teaching First Nations students has required a fundamental shift away from the expectations that Western models of learning have taught me to have of undergraduates. I've learned to accept things—mostly culturally based differences—that many of my colleagues have found annoying and unacceptable: students, running on "Indian time," who often show up late for class; cigarette breaks for classes that run longer than ninety minutes; and extensions, say, because a community needs one of its members, who happens to be one of my students, to make a ribbon shirt for the upcoming powwow or to help clean a moose. Perhaps most valuably, my teaching experiences have helped me to see the limitations of my pedagogical training, and have encouraged me to keep an open mind so that the experiences and values of others can help shape the kind of learning that takes place inside my classroom. Acknowledging my limitations, and making an effort to keep flexible, helps me to seek ways of making the classroom a more inclusive space for all students, particularly for those whom the university has not always done an excellent job of welcoming.

possible substitutes like "neocolonial" and "anticolonial," although I put it inside quotation marks in my title to denote the term's problematic status for those who are concerned about the homogenizing potential of an approach that tends to conceal the ongoing, specific challenges that many Aboriginal peoples face. Here in Manitoba, for example, there exists a documented need for at least 10,000 homes throughout the northern Aboriginal communities, while last year only about 170 were built. Native filmmaker and actor Michael Lawrenchuk's disturbing documentary, "As Long as the Sun Shines," details the living conditions in several of these communities where unemployment, suicide, poor health, and a lack of fresh water and sanitary living conditions continue to pose a severe threat to the well-being of many.

Works Cited

Astin, A.W. 1985. *Achieving Educational Excellence.* San Francisco: Jossey-Bass.

Baiocco, Sharon A. and Jamie N. DeWaters. 1998. *Successful College Teaching: Problem Solving Strategies of Distinguished Professors.* Boston: Allen & Bacon.

Campbell, Maria. 1973. *Halfbreed.* Toronto: McClelland and Stewart Ltd.

Clarke, Austin. 1998. "The Motor Car." In *The Harbrace Anthology of Literature,* 2nd edition, edited by Jon C. Stott, Raymond E. Jones, et al., 1113–26. New York: Harcourt Brace & Company.

"Cultural Clash Trims Students' Grades," *Winnipeg Free Press.* 10 January 2002.

Docker, John. 1995. "The Neocolonial Assumption in University Teaching of English." In *The Post-Colonial Studies Reader,* edited by Bill Ashcroft, Gareth Griffiths, and Helen Tiffin. London and New York: Routledge.

Erdrich, Louise. 1993. *Love Medicine.* New York: HarperPerennial.

King, Thomas. 1990. "Godzilla vs Postcolonial." *World Literature Written in English.* 30.2: 10–16.

Laurence, Margaret. 1998. "The Loons. "In *The Harbrace Anthology of Literature,* 2nd edition, edited by Jon C. Stott, Raymond E. Jones, et al., 1043–50. New York: Harcourt Brace & Company.

Lean, Arthur E. 1992. "The Farce Called 'Grading,'" repr. in. *75 Readings Plus,* edited by Santi Buscemi and Charlotte Smith, New York: McGraw-Hill, Inc.

Mukherjee, Bharati. 1998. "The Tenant. "In *The Harbrace Anthology of Literature,* 2nd edition, edited by Jon C. Stott, Raymond E. Jones, et al., 1152–62. New York: Harcourt Brace & Company.

Ruffo, Armand Garnet, ed. 2001. *(Ad)dressing Our Words: Aboriginal Perspectives on Aboriginal Literatures,* 233–42. Penticton, BC: Theytus Books.

Shapiro, Nancy S. and Jodi H. Levine. 1999. *Creating Learning Communities: A Practical Guide to Winning Support, Organizing for Change, and Implementing Programs.* San Francisco: Jossey-Bass.

Spivak, Gayatri Chakravorty. 1993. *Outside in the Teaching Machine.* New York and London: Routledge.

Tan, Amy. 1998. "Two Kinds." In *The Harbrace Anthology of Literature,* 2nd edition, edited by Jon C. Stott, Raymond E. Jones, et al., 1203–12. New York: Harcourt Brace & Company.

Walker, Alice. 1998. "Everyday Use." In *The Harbrace Anthology of Literature,* 2nd edition, edited by Jon C. Stott, Raymond E. Jones, et al., 1172–78. New York: Harcourt Brace & Company.

Warrior, Emma Lee. 1998. "Compatriots." In *An Anthology of Canadian Native Literature in English,* 2nd edition, edited by Daniel David Moses and Terry Goldie. 179–186. Oxford University Press.

Williams, William Carlos. 1998. "The Red Wheelbarrow." In *The Harbrace Anthology of Literature,* 2nd edition, edited by Jon C. Stott, Raymond E. Jones, et al., 287. New York: Harcourt Brace & Company.

8

Detecting the Camouflaged Conflicts

*Blackness, Whiteness, and Language Difference
in Basic Writing Courses*

Priscilla Perkins

Two weeks into an evening Basic Writing course, I was describing my response to a former acquaintance's racist comment when Michelle, an African-American computer science major, cut me short: "But Dr. Perkins, isn't that what white people usually talk about when they're alone: How much they hate black people?" Just like the racist remark that had prompted my story (intended to show how personal experience can influence critical analysis), Michelle's accusation momentarily paralyzed me. I knew I could count on five fingers the times I had heard such comments firsthand, and I had never remained friendly with someone who expressed racist sentiments.

Although I could not know it, Michelle's comment (which upset many of the students in this mixed group of African-Americans, European-Americans, and recent immigrants from India and Mexico) was both symptomatic and prophetic. Long after I'd forgotten the ensuing discussion, which I thought I had sensitively guided, their course evaluations documented the African-American students' memories of that night. They wrote that by telling my story and allowing the class to talk openly about racism, I had created a hostile atmosphere that interfered with black students' learning. Where I had seen the discussion as a spur to more integrated analysis of a subject that troubled us all, these students had described it as a demoralizing detour from the "proper" work of the course: attention to sentence-level correctness, dialect, and textual organization.

Were they right? My interactions with Michelle, which would seriously deteriorate during that semester, made me wonder. The course I taught had, as always, built skills through students' oral and written work with complex interdisciplinary readings. From the start, students knew they had to produce "clean" prose for the program-required, in-class final; if they did not pass the test, they repeated the course, the second time at the university's expense. My experiences working with African-American students, in particular, had led me to agree with Lisa Delpit's (2001) claim that "supporting students' transformation demands an extraordinary amount of time and commitment, but [that] teachers *can* make a difference if they are willing to make that commitment" (p. 550, emphasis in original). Aware of my responsibility to prepare students for the final—to "transform" their literacy practices in ways that would help them succeed academically, socially, and economically—I occasionally "taught to the test," especially when it came to the students' most disruptive sentence-level problems. This pragmatic pedagogy, however, was only partially effective when some students' cultural identities and personal experiences made them distrust their classmates' and instructor's motives. Because I underestimated the depth of Michelle's antagonism toward and anxiety about white, academic discourse (defined by James Paul Gee (2001) as "saying (writing)-doing-being-valuing-believing combinations" [p. 526]), I did not recognize Michelle's self-defeating attitude toward the course until it was too late for her to succeed. While I never would have substituted grammar drills for our life-based talk and writing, had I known what was on Michelle's mind, I would have offered even more support to her and other students who needed extra mechanical help in order to write their complex responses in the discourse that would let them through the university's various "gates." The only way I might have learned about this antagonism and anxiety, however, would have been to arrange a conference with Michelle shortly after our in-class confrontation. Caving in to my fear of reopening an apparently healing wound was perhaps my biggest mistake in the situation; since that semester, I have responded proactively to provocative behavior, sometimes even including a colleague and one of the student's classmates as more-or-less neutral witnesses to this kind of conference.

As her polarizing comment suggested, Michelle was a socially self-assured woman who had no qualms about putting other people on the spot. When travel for her job required her to miss several group revision sessions and three long, in-class writing exercises, she and her revision partners dutifully faxed their writing to each other and to me. Although I expressed misgivings about the value of her revision practices—she was rarely there to hear and respond to her partners' comments in person—she turned in reasonably strong work; between her articulate classroom persona and her first three essays, I had little worry that she would pass the course. After midsemester, however, her work changed. Her fourth essay, while just as readable as her first three, was woefully undeveloped. When I asked why, she replied that the readings were too tedious for her to work with. Given the engrossing writing that her peers had just produced, Michelle's response seemed strange, but I let it go: no set of readings intrigues every student. Then, three weeks before the exam, Michelle turned in an impromptu essay that was both analytically thin and filled with disruptive sentence boundary errors, subject–verb agreement problems, and the kinds of phrasing that suggest a writer's lack of comfort with Standard Edited English.

Rereading Michelle's in-class essay, several realities dawned on me, each one more upsetting than the last. Despite her ability to dominate discussion in a discourse that was generally appropriate to a college classroom, Michelle was far less experienced writing academic English than most of her peers were. With three classes left, her chances of passing Basic Writing were minuscule. Finally, I realized that her first three essays were not entirely her own work; while her revision partners were diligent (they had made great strides during the semester), both were Indian immigrants who could not have helped Michelle mold her accustomed modes of expression into the academically-polished essays I had graded. When I confronted Michelle, she revealed that her Anglo coworkers had edited and partly rewritten her first four essays. "You want me to write like a white person," she said, "but you stick me with people who can't write English at all. What did you expect me to do?"

The last two parts of Michelle's self-justification were easy to address. First, unless early semester experience has suggested that certain students will not work well together, I let students assemble their own revision groups; typical of adult students at my university, most of the class had quickly found collaborators that they trusted. Because Michelle's group seemed satisfied with the help they were giving each other, I had seen no reason to interfere. Second, of course, came the question of plagiarism: While these inexperienced college writers were unfamiliar with some aspects of academic integrity, they generally understood how their intraclass collaboration differed from less acceptable forms of assistance. Michelle's original assertion still troubled me. Did I expect her to "write white" in order to pass? In class, I had expressed support for the students' right to their own language, but we also explored "code-switching," the practice of adapting one's speech and writing to suit the demands of home, workplace, and classroom. The students (including Michelle, I thought) had seemed to recognize that our brief grammar lessons and one-on-one consultations offered them discursive tools, while class discussions and writing assignments provided secure opportunities to practice new codes.

Looking back, I believe that their own or their families' previous experiences with racism, overt and subtle, may have led African-American students to misinterpret (or perhaps overinterpret) some of their classmates' and my comments. Because Michelle had aired her racial assumptions so early and openly, I could not know how much more distrust—both of non-black students and of the educational process itself—she and her black peers held on to. In the months after that semester, I worried that simply introducing the idea of code-switching had sent students like Michelle the wrong message; since then, however, I have been much more vocal about the necessity of learning how to code-switch. As Lisa Delpit (2001) writes,

> the open acknowledgment of ["discourse-stacking"] in the very institution that facilitates the sorting process is liberating in itself. . . . Only after acknowledging the inequity of the system can the teacher's stance then be

"Let me show you how to cheat!" And of course, to cheat is to learn the
discourse which would otherwise be used to exclude them from participating
in and transforming the mainstream. (p. 554)

In order to keep the learning environment as comfortable as possible for all
students—especially socially vulnerable African Americans—I have talked
up this kind of "cheating" mostly in the context of one-on-one meetings.

Again, thinking back to that stressful semester, I have also come to think
that the ethnic makeup of our class put an unexpected twist on the messages
that we exchanged. Ideal as the rough three-way balance of this class had orig-
inally seemed, I later saw that nearly equalizing the ratios of white, black, and
immigrant students in a course did not even out the shadows that the extramu-
ral social facts of Chicago life—segregated housing, racist violence, lopsided
educational opportunities in these students' precollege years—cast on everything we did. In a class of mostly African-American students, the familiar notion of code-switching might have seemed less politically loaded; we could
have conspired openly, as Delpit advocates, to master the rules of white discourse. As it was, the black students recognized that their white classmates
faced fewer demands to switch linguistic registers; the language they used at
home was not dramatically different from the languages they used elsewhere.
Immigrant students, eager to snag office jobs, rarely disguised their strong desires to master dominant codes. Despite my naive efforts to craft a message that
would speak to every subject position in the classroom, Michelle and her
African-American peers probably saw themselves as targets of discriminatory
double-speak: while I claimed to value the language practices they brought
with them, I seemed also to demand that they quickly adopt the practices their
white classmates had absorbed over the course of two or three decades. For her
part, Michelle simultaneously claimed (with more than a hint of nativism) that
I was too patient with ESL students: because their writing was demonstrably
"worse" than that of the black students, she said, the immigrants should all
have to repeat the course, regardless of the development their writing showed.

In the last three weeks of the semester, I tried to recapture lost time with
Michelle. These were tense sessions. My refusal simply to rewrite Michelle's
sentences and essays led her to painful reproaches: "At least the white people
at work *want* to help me. You're just confusing me and keeping me down." As
I feverishly coached her for the final exam and then, discouraged, reviewed her
failing effort with colleagues, I wondered how Michelle's white coworkers had
influenced the choices she made about her work in the course. Assuming she
was right in saying that they were more invested in her success than I was
(which I still doubt), I wondered whether she was in college to "remediate"
language practices that interfered with her job performance, or was simply
jumping through a corporate hoop her white coworkers had already passed. If
college was just a hoop, then perhaps her coworkers' "help" represented some
version of corporate teamwork: Because Michelle was a valued member of

their group, they helped her finish her—their—"project" on schedule and on budget. If, on the other hand, her coworkers were pointedly aware of the differences between their writing and her own, maybe they saw their contributions as a gesture toward cultural inclusiveness. They did not want her career harmed because of nebulous social standards that they participated in, but neither created nor controlled.

Thinking about Michelle's two "white" language communities made me wonder whose prescriptions—the corporation's or the university's—carried the most weight in her world. Although the aims of these institutionally "white" constituencies overlapped, they were not identical; in important ways, as my refusal to rewrite Michelle's essays shows, they opposed each other. This insight (combined with her demand that the university establish racially segregated writing courses "so that black students won't get ripped off anymore") made it impossible for me to accept Michelle's generalizations about "what white people do" and "what white people think." Now, as I continue to reflect on the intricacies of race and writing pedagogy, I am more aware of the limitations of "whiteness" as a broad explanatory construct. I also know the puzzling powers of black and white people to undermine each other with "support," and to support each other when we appear most to be adversaries. Possibilities for both kinds of action are everywhere; what we need is to stay alert for signs of the camouflaged conflicts, and to act courageously and thoughtfully on what we see.

Works Cited

Cushman, Ellen, Eugene R. Kintgen, Barry M. Kroll, and Mike Rose. 2001. *Literacy: A Critical Sourcebook.* Boston: Bedford–St. Martin's.

Delpit, Lisa. 2001. "The Politics of Teaching Literate Discourse." In *Literacy: A Critical Sourcebook,* edited by Ellen Cushman, Eugene R. Kintgen, Barry M. Kroll, and Mike Rose, 545–54. Boston: Bedford–St. Martin's.

Gee, James Paul. 2001. "Literacy, Discourse, and Linguistics: Introduction *and* What Is Literacy?" In *Literacy: A Critical Sourcebook,* edited by Ellen Cushman, Eugene R. Kintgen, Barry M. Kroll, and Mike Rose, 525–44. Boston: Bedford–St. Martin's.

9

"What's the Point?"

Stephen Dilks

The point is not simply that, since our racial [add "and any other"] differences do not constitute all of us, we are always different, negotiating different kinds of differences—of gender, of sexuality, of class [add "etcetera"]. It is that these antagonisms refuse to be neatly aligned; they are simply not reducible to one another; they refuse to coalesce around a single axis of differentiation. We are always in negotiation, not with a single set of oppositions that place us always in the same relation with others, but with a series of different positionalities. Each has for us its point of profound subjective identification. (Hall, 1996, p. 473)

On Day One of a required "Writing Intensive" class called "Theory and Practice of Composition," Ward Sears publicly challenged me to make it worth his while to continue with the course: "What are you going to teach me? . . . Why the heck am I required to take this course?" His conversational abrasiveness was matched by his prose. In his first essay, "Bizzell Bites the Dust," Sears dismissed Pat Bizzell's (1985) "Academic Discourse and Critical Consciousness" as a "fine example of the mastery of the art of blathering" and as a "cesspool of prattle." But this disarming lack of respect was accompanied by a charming stubbornness and persistence. Throughout the semester, Sears returned to the question that formed the basis of his blunt critical appraisal of Bizzell and Paulo Freire: "Does academia function to create enlightened masses or is it simply there to create more academics?" His own pragmatic answer was articulated on the first day; and he repeated his blunt appraisal of academic work in his first essay: "Generally, a student takes a class so he can acquire a certain knowledge with which he can be accepted into a certain community and/or get a job." The challenge Sears presents to teachers who identify with progressive pedagogies that are energized by complex understandings of essayism and multiculturalism was immediately evident: How do we teach anything other than strict formalism in the face of students who insist that an English class should teach basic skills and conventions? How do we maintain what bell hooks (1994) calls "an unbiased inclusive perspective" (p. 43) in the face of an obnoxious, deliberately rude white guy with deer-blood on his jacket and Missouri mud ingrained into his labor-cracked hands?

Not much younger than I, wearing an attitude that would stop conversation in a bar in Portland, Missouri, Sears asserted himself with the brash honesty of someone who is sick and tired of useless education. Somehow his questions were a reaction against my introduction, a deliberately essayistic ramble designed to illustrate connections between and among personal, academic, and cultural experiences and assumptions. Beginning by noting that the class emphasized interactions between theory and practice and that I would do my best to teach them ways to negotiate between personal experience, academic discourse, and cultural phenomena, I explained that I'd learned about language and composition from Samuel Beckett, James Joyce, Gertrude Stein, and Virginia Woolf. I then tried to show how these lessons became personally meaningful in the context of my own lived experience. And I suggested that everything I do as a teacher and writer is connected with my departure from Lincolnshire, in the wake of Thatcherism and the war in the Falklands/Malvinas, in an idealistic search for true social democracy. I'd also explained my belief that education is about learning to engage in productive, healing, meaningful conversations with anyone, anywhere: The tale of my journeys from Cyprus and the Cyclades to Stirlingshire, Kansas and Paris, and from New Jersey and Thessalonika to North Dakota and Kansas City was intended to suggest the importance of nonacademic influences in my intellectual development *and* to complicate perceptions of my "Englishness." This interweaving of personal tales with academic influences and cultural observations was designed to demonstrate my commitment to essayism, to a process of creative and critical associativeness that responds to intertextuality and interdiscursivity, engaging the personal, institutional, and cultural situatedness of academic readers and writers. True to my developing theory of essayism, I was responsive to the geographic and historical situation we were in, in a particular classroom in Kansas City, Missouri: I introduced the concept of "perennial polyculture," an adaptation of Wes Jackson's (1987) term (in *Altars of Unhewn Stone: Science and the Earth*) for the prairie-based, soil-sensitive work being done at The Land Institute in Salina, Kansas, and Matfield Green, a few hours drive west of our campus.[1] Following Jackson's "search for the unifying concept for sustainable agriculture" (p. 81) through the planting of multiple crops

---

1. Jackson's term is "the polyculture of perennials." In the essay, "Living Nets in a New Prairie Sea" (in *Altars of Unhewn Stone,* 1987), Jackson discusses " the opportunity to develop a truly sustainable agriculture based on the polyculture of perennials." (81)

in shared soil, I set out to explain and demonstrate a method for teaching independent critical research based on the essayistic interaction between and among different orders of cognition and expression that are rooted in local conditions and contexts: and I concluded by pointing to the course description and syllabus, telling them that the entire course was designed to elucidate and explore, to inhabit and practice, different kinds of essayism.

But Sears gave me a long, hard stare and said, "Okay, very interesting, but what's the point of this class?" In a moment, my pedagogy seemed about as useful as a computer on Robinson Crusoe's island. But, by taking Sears' seriously, within a few more moments I began to learn, and to teach, valuable lessons about relationships between prescribed pedagogies and real-time classroom experiences, between approaches that preimagine the classroom community, formulating syllabi and assignments before the course has begun, and approaches that actively respond to the immediate social conditions and dramas that characterize and energize a specific social gathering. What is, perhaps, most instructive about the situation I am describing is that my conscious commitment to an organicist, context-specific pedagogy was overwhelmed during my explanation of this pedagogy by what I can only call a "default" mechanism, a mechanism that transformed everything I said into academic abstraction, teacherly posturing, intellectual elitism. Puncturing the balloon of teacherliness with his brash style, in that first class, Sears began to teach me to be more responsive to extant conditions, to be less dependent on abstract notions of an imagined community. There are, then, three points to this essay: First, teachers must let themselves change their minds' in response to specific classroom situations; second, teachers must both admit and publicly analyze these changes of mind; and, in the long run and after long reflection, I learned a third point: effective pedagogies allow for the constant renegotiation of relationships between extant and imagined conditions and contexts.

Six weeks after Day One, in an essay called "Creation from Conflict," Sears had begun to reflect on his ornery attitude toward me and the academy: "At one point, Bizzell comments on students' efforts to retain 'their own' language in their developing stages as writers, emphasizing the conflict between the establishment and those who are trying to enter it or at the very least 'take' something from it." While he continued to write about this conflict in terms of a "collision," Sears had begun to develop a theory that took account of academia's social and cultural contexts. Contentious as he remained, Sears ultimately developed a compelling, although profoundly conservative, critique of Bizzell and Freire: "Perhaps more attention should be paid to the requirements of the job market and how to teach to that end than what it takes to be 'free' students."

Sears raised a number of personal, professional, and political issues during the course of the semester and, despite his insistence on functionality, he began to complicate his (and my) understanding of utility and what he liked to call "fou-fou" or "academic bull." A number of the issues he raised involved him in glaring contradictions and it was these contradictions that led both to heated in-class debates and to more complex thinking/writing. For example, his monologues and disruptions often amounted to an insistence that students respect teachers by listening: an immediate, in-the-moment rejection of teacherliness competed with a powerful tendency to survive by voicing abstract respect for teaching as a profession. In short, then, the dissonance between rebellion and obeisance became the main source of progress for Sears as a student and for me as a teacher. Analyzing a personal experience in a speech class where he had been penalized for transgressing the rules, Sears argued that it was time "to revise my presentations to suit the parameters of the course, hopefully receiving better marks and 'survive' the course." But he did so in an essay that made clear his preference for the less formal, more experimental style of public speaking used in his work as a guide at the Fort Osage Historic site. On the one hand he expressed the deliberately "safe" view that personal ways of thinking must be excised from academic prose, arguing that academic discourse is "devoid of any personal meaning or satisfaction." Sears, a student consciously endeavoring to improve his class position by adapting "[his] conduct in order to survive academically," rejected progressive pedagogies designed to enable non-mainstream students like himself, transforming Adrienne Rich's (2002) feminist perspective in her essay "When We Dead Awaken: Writing as Re-Vision" into a cynical argument in favor of accommodation to "the academic environment." The speech class had confirmed that it is a mistake to "test . . . boundaries," teaching him that academe issues valid passports only to those who "suit the parameters." Academic survival was becoming, for Sears, a matter of formal accommodation to default positions; and the main characteristic of the default position was that it required the erasure of personal and political engagement with the immediate, extant environment. While I persisted in defining the class in terms of a theory that revises and expands academic discourse so as to incorporate aspects of personal and cultural situatedness, it gradually became apparent that, after the gunsmoke cleared, Sears was increasingly inclined to see education as a matter of professional training. Fortunately, however, the story is more interesting.

Repositioning

Three years after I received the final essay from Ward Sears, "An Examination of Osage Language Sources," I am staring at a mottled, creamy, ash-encrusted bar of soap made from rendered tallow and a bag of dehydrated red-corn wrapped in a modified Osage recipe for hominy. Ward Sears gave me these gifts and he taught me how to cook hominy over a fire dug into the ground and how to light a fire with a flint and charred cotton. During the meal, eaten in the damp, smoky gloom of an afternoon in November on a bluff overlooking the Missouri River, someone discharged an early nineteenth century muzzle-loading rifle. The shockingly loud bang punctuated a lesson in active research with a reminder of the foremost instrument of power in the decades before Frederick Jackson Turner announced the closing of the American frontier. With the reconstructed trading post and battlements of Fort Osage as his backdrop, Sears gave life to stories in *Pioneer Women, Mapping the Farm,* and *Native American Testimony,* quoting my theories about interactions between personal expression, academic discourse, and cultural critique, challenging me to explain our situation in terms of "autoethnography" and "transculturation," mimicking the dry academic language of Composition theorists, teaching a sequence of Osage signs, cutting techniques, methods of farming and cooking and hunting, and then explaining how the fort functioned through summers and winters in the 1820s. To the list of nonacademic educational experiences that have influenced my work as a teacher I could now add the experience of cooking and eating, staying warm and trading goods, in conditions akin to those familiar to pre-1850s pioneers in Missouri.

But let's return to that first day of class. The loud, no-nonsense voice with which Sears announced that he had had enough of boring lectures and stupid discussions had almost provoked me, on our first meeting, to say, "If you don't want to be here, then leave!" (or words to that effect). Instead I hesitated, decided to take a risk, and said, "Look, my first instinct as a teacher is to say to you, 'Ward, as a person, if you don't like the class, leave'; but perhaps we can try a different approach—why don't you form groups of three and discuss Ward's question—what do the rest of you expect to get out of this class?" Conscious that Sears was responding to me as a teacher, not to me as a person, I deflected his challenge in a way that kept the road clear for him to spend a semester thinking about relationships between and among personal opinions, academic conventions, and political exigencies. A question designed to provoke an exclusive dialogue that could only have led to oppositional inflexibility was transformed into a question that opened an energetic conversation among peers. Clearly, I already knew that lessons in critical consciousness begin with the teacher's ability to re-direct student energy even when this energy is hostile. But I relearned this lesson in a hands-on way, recognizing the value in techniques that dramatize differences between individuals and the class of people they supposedly represent (Englishmen, red-necks, students, teachers, etc.).

From Day One, Sears's challenge to my authority and my deflection of this challenge into a peer discussion about the purpose of "The Theory and Practice of Composition," helped to create an atmosphere in the classroom where students felt free to challenge what we were doing in the full expectation that they'd be taken seriously: interruptions became a source of fruitful digressions; highly personal reactions became a way of complicating our various imagined communities; dialogue about what we would do, as a class, became a routine performed at the outset of each period. The concept of "polycultural perennialism" became a material practice. On that first day, instead of blathering about my idea that any given classroom should cultivate personal expression, academic discourse, and political analysis, I tried an experiment and left the room, letting students cross-fertilize their ideas without my direct intervention. After I had revealed the dissonance between my urge to rid myself of a potential source of headaches and my belief that education begins with conflict, I said, "Use the syllabus I just handed out to think about Ward's question in terms of what you hope this class will do for you, your job prospects, and your understanding of culture." Then I left, returning after twenty minutes to dismiss the class. This produced the first new lesson for me: Early in the semester, on Day One if the occasion arises, it is good for the teacher to leave the students to their own devices. As students become comfortable expressing views that may well be unfashionable in contexts regulated by academic authority, they become more willing to express these views when the teacher is in the room. Essayism, which is always on the verge of becoming yet another default option in the repertoire of academic conventions, becomes part of lived classroom experience. We know full well that students are perennially good at mimicking views and opinions that are acceptable to the teacher: this process of reproduction becomes much more intellectually engaged when the pursuit of points-of-view deemed "intellectually responsible" is put in the hands of a student and her/his peers. We can complicate the writing process by insisting that all views and opinions are acceptable so long as they are presented in the context of essayistic explorations that weave personal, academic, and cultural experiences and theories, but we always risk a return to default, automatic, "safe" responses when we allow any given model of understanding to dominate classroom discourse.

In the corridor, still off balance in response to a direct attack and still unsure about my quick decision to defuse the situation by assigning a task for discussion and then leaving, I worked out an answer to Sears' question: "What's the point?"

The point is to learn portable, usable, adaptable knowledge, knowledge with meaningful connections beyond any given classroom situation and, by extension, beyond the constraints of any given professional, cultural, or political situation. Educators who define themselves and certain students as "problem-posers" in opposition to those who have not yet seen the light, take on themselves the arrogant task of demystifying students and colleagues who are already fully equipped with their own forms of critical consciousness. My experience with Sears underscores the need to avoid Freirian reductiveness and to shift the emphasis from prescriptive political agendas to complex essayistic explorations that directly respond to immediate circumstances. And it underscores the importance of Stuart Hall (1996) in the revision of student–teacher relations. We do an injustice to any specific participant in academe if we fail to accept that, as Hall puts it, the various "antagonisms" within academia "refuse to be neatly aligned; they are simply not reducible to one another; they refuse to coalesce around a single axis of differentiation." We fail ourselves, as teacher–students and student–teachers, if we fail to recognize that "We are always in negotiation, not with a single set of oppositions that place us always in the same relation with others, but with a series of different positionalities" (Hall, 1996, p. 473). By upsetting the applecart, by being rude and obnoxious and unapologetically committed to self-improvement, by demanding that the course cater to his narrowly defined, job-oriented objectives, and by presenting himself to me and his peers as a no-nonsense hick from rural Missouri, Sears interrupted my lesson plan, forcing me and the other participants in "The Theory and Practice of Composition" to recognize that the classroom is a social space that requires the constant renegotiation of discursive and behavioral practices. If only we admit it, we each arrive at any given class-period unbalanced by the various antagonisms and differentiations that give us our positions in the world, in the academy, in the specific social group that congregates in a specified time and place in order that a specific kind of learning might happen. Hall lets us see that the politics of identification and transformation are much more complicated than Freirian critique allows; Hall encourages us to use antagonisms and differentiations as a catalyst for the experience of actively engaged, context-specific explorations.

And this leads to my final point. Sears helped me see that specific political agendas and pedagogies, even those that are deliberately "inclusivist," are much less effective in making education meaningful to all-comers than approaches that dramatize dissonances between different ways of thinking about any given situation. We all arrive carrying what we carry, whether it be a theory that is designed to make the writer responsible for working out her/his own ways of mediating between and among personal experience, academic discourse, and cultural critique, or whether it be a specific, increasingly cynical understanding of what it means to "survive" in the educational system. But if we are to learn about teaching *with* students like Ward Sears, students who appear to be graced with white, male privilege but who are too rural and too ornery to take advantage of these privileges, we must not only help them identify and explore the places where their subjective and culturally embedded assumptions already reproduce *and* transgress the conventions of the academy. But we must also let them learn to read situations with sufficient attention to competing discourses to appreciate when and where survival depends on conformity. But we abdicate our responsibilities if we try to do so through prescriptive pedagogies and default attitudes; or, to put it another way, we teach context-specific discourse practices more effectively when, instead of advocating specific pedagogies and attitudes, we dramatize and analyze different ways of responding to different situations and when, instead of comfortably inhabiting the role of "teacher," we let ourselves learn, suspending what we have already figured out by responding directly and actively to the situation before us. Active literacy may well gain its fullest expression in essayistic prose driven by the dynamic interaction between and among personal experiences, academic discourses, and cultural positionings. But teacherly advocacy and demonstration of this theory often has the effect of deactivating students because the teacher's prelearned theory begins to function as a prescriptive model (even when this theory is deliberately antiprescriptivist). We must, then, expose and dramatize the ways in which we change our minds, openly rethinking relationships between what we thought we'd be teaching and what we actually find ourselves teaching. We must expose and analyze the ways in which we reposition ourselves in response to students, revealing and discussing the ways in which we make things up as we go along. If we are prepared to do so, we create educational environments that reinforce two fundamental educational principles: It's okay to change one's mind, and it's okay to engage in open discussion of such changes.

Works Cited

Bizzell, Pat. 1992. "Academic Discourse and Critical Consciousness." Pittsburgh, PA: University of Pittsburgh Press.

Freire, Paulo. 1985. *The Politics of Education: Culture Power and Liberation.* Translated by Donald Macedo. New York: Bergin and Garvey.

Hall, Stuart. 1996. "What Is this 'Black' in Black Popular Culture?" In *Stuart Hall: Critical Dialogues in Cultural Studies,* edited by David Morley and Kuan-Hsing Chen. New York: Routledge.

hooks, bell. 1994. *Teaching to Transgress: Education as the Practice of Freedom.* New York: Routledge.

Jackson, Wes. 1987. *Altars of Unhewn Stone: Science and the Earth.* New York: North Point Press.

Rich, Adrienne. 2002. "When We Dead Awaken: Writing as Re-Vision." In *Ways of Reading: An Anthology for Writers,* 6th edition, edited by David Bartholomae and Anthony Petrosky 627–640. Boston: Bedford St. Martin's.

10

Pedagogy and Apocalypse

How to Have a Productive Discussion
in the Context of a Race Riot

T. R. Johnson

In early June 1992, no more than a month after Los Angeles had erupted in widespread rioting to protest the acquittal of the police officers who beat Rodney King, I met for the first time a section of English 101 that I had been assigned to teach at the University of Louisville during the short summer term. I walked into class that first day, distributed the syllabus, and started reading off the roster of names—the usual routine for the first day of the semester. Almost instantly, however, something seemed terribly wrong. Then it hit me. At one edge of the classroom, three rows of desks had been filled by white students, and, against the opposite wall, three rows had been filled by black students. In the middle of the classroom stood a painfully symbolic eight or ten rows of desks that were completely empty. I tried to stand in the center of the room, but it was impossible to address the class without turning awkwardly to face one way and then the other. What's worse, I could hardly speak at all because I kept inwardly agonizing over how long I was looking toward one side or the other. The air was heavy with the two groups' mutual outrage, and all eyes were on me. I stammered, "L-let's all move toward the center and p-put our desks in a circle." One kid on one side of the room (I don't remember which), immediately declared, "I'm not moving." And in almost the same instant, another on the opposite side simply blurted, "Nope!"

"See," I said, "you guys have already shown you can agree on something. So, let's start there." Nobody laughed. A strange, even explosive moment. In the back of my mind—and, most likely, everyone else's too—were the rumors that had been flying around campus earlier that morning about a new student who had shown up for orientation the previous day with a loaded pistol.

I cleared my throat. Everyone in the room seemed to anticipate violence. "Take out a sheet of paper, please," I said. As they did so, a strong wave of relief rolled through me. "Please write about what you hope to gain from this class, and also what your biggest fears are about this class." I was temporarily off the hook. I've always liked to have students write from this prompt on the first day, because, reading their responses later, I get a sense of "where they're at" and, too, I like to return these writings to them on the last day of the semester and use them as the basis for discussing how their writing—and, in particular, how their sense of what learning to write entails—has changed.

I was especially inclined to use this exercise that day, however, because I was worried about how to start a discussion. In the past, whenever a discussion wasn't going particularly well, I would have my students free-write for five or ten minutes in response to some particular prompt and then put them in groups to discuss what they wrote. I would then ask them to pin down at least one connection between each others' material and at least one point of difference. And then the small groups would report to the large group, and a relatively more compelling discussion would follow naturally from there. It had always helped get discussions going in the past, but this time I would need to move much more slowly. After all, I was not just struggling with a fairly lifeless discussion; I was facing a class that had constituted itself, in its opening moment, around an absolute refusal to have any sort of peaceful interaction.

As the students wrote, my mind raced. *What should I do next? I can't simply have them free-write for every class meeting all semester! What am I going to do? They won't talk to each other—there's too much rage.* I was on the verge of panic. I knew, however, that if I began to panic, I would jeopardize the entire semester.

For several years, I had built my pedagogy around student discussion. From a variety of sources, I had come to believe that when students exchange perspectives and negotiate positions, they're stimulated to generate better and better ideas for their writing. What's more, they become more attuned to each other as audiences for each others' written work. In a more abstract sense, the more students speak with each other and with me in a public and formal way, the more they internalize this dialogue and thereby begin to converse within themselves about their ideas and their texts—in short, class discussion, as Kenneth Bruffee (1984) argues, forms the cognitive foundation for critical reflection. Also, as students absorb and explore perspectives other than their own, they not only mature socially and cognitively and learn to think critically, but they also acquire a broader repertoire of voices to borrow from and imitate. As Joseph Harris (1996) suggests, this sense of voice as plural and external can prove essential to developing real rhetorical skill (p. 34). Moreover, this sort of forum, I had always felt, helps to make the world itself, in a tiny but meaningful way, more tolerant of diversity, more respectful of difference. In sum, I've always sensed that something more or less magical in the ordinary rhythms of speech, something akin to music, and, just as good music makes us want to dance, good conversation prompts our thoughts to leap, twist, and weave new perspectives; more broadly, as Walter Ong (1982) suggests, the dimension of orality, of sound, helps to soften the boundaries of the individual self in ways that sight doesn't. In fact, psychoanalytic theorists like Jacques Lacan and Shoshana Felman (1987) would agree with Ong's more phenomenological accout: Conversation is the life-blood of learning, and, for that matter, the lifeblood of all the many forms of progress any classroom seeks to achieve (see Felman, 1987, p. 29).

But on that first day of the summer session of 1992, the mood, to put it mildly, was not inclined to progress. Good conversations weren't going to happen anytime soon. I would have to teach this class—or at least the first two or three weeks of it—without any discussion. But how? I love to lecture, but that method is singularly inappropriate for a writing class. I would have to come up with something. After a few more minutes of writing, I collected their papers and proceeded to introduce the books for the course and talk about the workload and general policies and so forth, and then I let the class go about fifteen minutes early.

I went back to my office and started reading through the nervously scrawled paragraphs my students had submitted. Nothing particularly unusual there. A few of them, though, did express the predictable sentiments in ways that were fresh and catchy, and I found myself copying them out in a notebook and writing the name of the student who wrote it underneath the lines I had quoted. Then an idea came: I would type up five or six quotes from this pile of papers with the author's name under each, photocopy them, distribute them in class, and use them as the basis for a kind of mini-lecture about the themes that they raised. I had seen the same technique work wonderfully in a seminar on Composition Theory that I took from James Slevin at the University of Virginia a few years earlier. Like Slevin, I wouldn't plot my lecture in great detail, for that sort of formality and stiffness, I suspected, would only exacerbate the gulf that seemed to stretch between me and my much divided students. Rather, I would use their quotes as notes and simply improvise from there. That, I hoped, would keep my tone lively and engaging and thereby begin the tricky process of getting this class off the ground.

The process worked. The students seemed surprised to see their own names and their own remarks in print, and quite proud. The written document seemed to create an atmosphere of dignity and accountability that was precisely the opposite of the apocalyptic possibilities that had seethed among them before I distributed the quotes. People were still jumpy, but a kind of window had opened, one that seemed to invite a very different "vibe." That window was simply the piece of paper full of student quotes, and that vibe, again, although full of the energy of all-out riot, had focused itself on words and what they meant. No one could ascertain with confidence the race of the person making the assertion in the quote, and so I managed to suspend, at least for the time being, the ugly binary that otherwise held the class in check. For homework that night, I assigned them some reading (if memory serves, it was Mike Rose's (1998) "I Just Wanna Be Average," from the popular textbook, *Rereading*

America) and, in class the next day, I asked them to free-write again from a series of prompts. That night, I culled maybe ten quotes from their writing, but this time I grouped the quotes according to theme so that I had two or three quotes on each of a couple of issues. Again, each quote was followed by the name of its author, and no one could quite be sure who was who. At the end of the series of quotes, I posed questions that sought to extend and elaborate the ideas floating around in the quoted material above them. These questions would be prompts for more writing the next day. I repeated the method for the first several class-meetings, and the mood lightened considerably. The class is still characterized by a degree of relative solemnity, but rather than taking the form of an outright refusal to communicate, it has shifted into something like a deep yearning to communicate carefully and well.

Through this method, I was able to generate a discussion, but one that happened exclusively in written form. The "discussion" thereby took on a certain formality and rigor that it probably wouldn't have had otherwise. Also, students whose names and ideas appeared on the sheet enjoyed a real ego boost, while, somewhat paradoxically, their anonymity was partially protected by the fact that no one had yet been able to attach faces (and, most importantly, races) to anyone's name. Over the first few weeks of class, I made certain to quote each student at least once, and, as I began to stage certain dialogic configurations between the quotes, I deliberately brought white and black students into unwitting contact. After the third week of this, I was ready to assign a more ambitious, much longer paper and I went so far as to make this first paper a collaborative assignment. I used obvious connections between student quotes as the basis for forming the groups, and, thus, "inevitably" white students and black students were in the same group.

Things went quite well. More specifically, I found that because the students had first begun to interact, verbally, within the formal codes of written speech, their interaction in groups had a seriousness, a professionalism, and a maturity that I know would never have appeared on its own. The students also seemed to be energized by the experience of working closely with each other, as if the antipathy that had colored their first meeting had been somehow sublimated into rigorous intellectual exchange. Both black and white students seemed quietly delighted to find themselves interacting this way, and, as I recall, the papers they generated were much stronger than most early-in-the-semester projects usually are.

I learned a number of things as I taught this class, especially during those nervous first few weeks. For starters, the expressivist notion that strong, useful writing is writing that stays close to a "self," or manifests a distinctive personal identity would seem quite false, for it was precisely in their relative anonymity that my students found a way to communicate with each other at all. With the wide availability now of computer technology, the implication that follows this insight is that an email listserv would be an extraordinarily effective tool to use in conjunction with a writing classroom. Another important lesson here is that a great deal can be gained from writing during class time. Indeed, in a purely oral exchange, some students can drift off or withdraw from the loop, they can shyly retire to the rear of the classroom to doze under a baseball cap or a curtain of long hair, but, if everyone has to write and hand the writing in, no one can fail completely to gain anything from the class. Yet another lesson—and perhaps this one is the most important—is that no matter how disastrous a classroom situation appears, it can always be saved by simply having your students write and by doing something clever with the writing that they produce.

Works Cited

Bruffee, Kenneth. 1984. "Collaborative Learning and the Conversation of Mankind." *College English* 46.7 (November): 635–52.

Felman, Shoshana. 1987. *Jacques Lacan and the Adventure of Insight: Psychoanalysis in Contemporary Culture.* Cambridge: Harvard University Press.

Harris, Joseph. 1996. *A Teaching Subject: Composition Since 1966.* Upper Saddle River: Prentice Hall.

Ong, Walter. 1982. *Literarcy and Orality: The Technologizing of the Word.* London: Methuen, 1982.

Rose, Mike. 2002. "I Just Wanna Be Average." In *Rereading America: Cultural Contexts for Critical Reading and Writing,* 4th edition, edited by Gary Colombo, Robert Cullen and Bonnie Lisle, 174–185. Boston: Bedford/St. Martins.

11

Race in Class

Students, Teaching, and Stories

Linda Adler-Kassner

> Whenever a continuity is desired, a frame can be established that
> will inevitably valorize certain information and devalue other infor-
> mation. More often than not, inquiring subjects "frame" their field of
> inquiry according to accepted and acceptable modes of framing.
> —Laurie Edson, *Reading Relationally* (2000, p. 4)

In his essay in this collection, Hugh English (2003) suggests that the "difficult moments" faced by instructors are difficult not only because of the challenge that they
present for the immediate time, but because they can also shake the foundations of
a course—of a teacher's carefully constructed persona, of the "communities" that
they/we try to create in our classrooms, of the power relationships that we construct (and/or try to represent in nonthreatening ways) in our work (see p. 119). The
perceptions of students—held by students *and* by instructors—in basic writing
classes add a layer to the potential for these difficult moments. Particularly in programs where placement in basic writing courses lays outside of the students' control, the emotions and intellectual experiences that students bring to the course can
result in especially complex classroom situations. My experience with a student
named "Ted" represented one of these difficult moments, and I describe his story
and my attempts to work with it—and him—below. However, I think that Laurie
Edson's epigraph also has much to offer to instructors as they consider stories like
these; thus, I also explore a number of interpretations of the "Ted" moment and
consider the implications both of using such stories, and of this story, as well.

Ted

In 1998–99, I spent time interviewing students who placed into basic writing
classes like the one in which Ted, a student in my fall course, was enrolled. One

of the conclusions I'd reached from these interviews was that basic writing teachers must be more accountable to students placed in these classes. For me, this meant designing a curriculum that asked students to investigate questions related to definitions of writing and literacy in our own institutional context. The assignment sequence in the course reflected the assumptions I made about the course and about students. In the first paper, I asked students to identify a problem or question related to education and/or literacy that was important to them, and write about why it was important. As a model, we read and closely analyzed the first two chapters of *Lives on the Boundary,* where Mike Rose (1989) poses questions and problems he sees in the educational system and moves onto his own experiences growing up in Los Angeles. Because Rose isn't explicit about the links between these things, this was a challenge for students, but by wrestling with the text, they made it a workable model. Next, in the second paper, students worked with a set of photographs and texts to identify what they believed to be the purpose of education and literacy. The assignment involved a number of choices; as students made these and wrote about why they chose as they had, they narrowed their purposes and grounded them in specific, concrete experiences. After this work, they returned to the first essay, now posted on a shared, online class space, to choose a question or a problem they wanted to investigate in their third paper. Through a long, guided process they collected evidence from a number of sources—official institutional documents, interviews, mainstream news sources, each other, previous readings and writing—to address questions like, "How are placement exams written and scored?" and "What do high school and college teachers see as the purpose of writing in college?" In the last paper before the portfolio revisions, finally, students either created a document for a specific audience based on their work in the third essay, or they wrote a more traditional paper on what they believed should be the purpose of education and literacy based on their work.

The assumptions I made through all of this are probably clear: Basic writing courses should be places for students to learn about and, if they want to, weigh in on institutional practices that affect them; students should be exposed to the potential that writing holds outside of the classroom, and at least consider how "classroom" writing might extend beyond that space. Most important for this essay are the assumptions I made about students: Students are smart; they *must* find ways to make writing meaningful for them; the instructor (me) must provide guidance and helpful structure so that they can tackle big questions. My approach then, as now, was to set up meaningful challenges, then to believe in students and work hard *with* students to achieve them. The key word for me was *support*—support opportunities for smart ideas, support their development, support the writing. But as the fall 1999 semester developed, one student, whom I'll call "Ted," presented challenges to this approach.

Ted was an African-American student who had just graduated from a Detroit high school. He made a point of demonstrating how attentive and responsible he was at the beginning of the semester, sitting in the front row and always participating actively in small- and large-group discussions. He also intervened in what I think of as "teacherly" ways with other students in the class. If someone was having a problem with a computer, for instance, he would jump to their assistance, instantly fixing it (rather than showing them how to do so, as I might have done).

About three weeks into the semester, Ted disappeared. After he had been gone for over two weeks, I assumed that he had dropped the class. Shortly after, however, he returned more determined than ever. He insisted that he would be in class from that day forward, that he would have his work done, and that he was committed to the class. At the same time, he began telling me what a terrific writer he was. (At this point I had seen only two in-class assignments and a long essay draft from him; he had missed a considerable amount of additional writing work in his absence.) When I pulled him aside to talk about my comments on his first essay—which was in need of development, as first essays often are—he told me that this really didn't show his writing strengths.

As the class went on, Ted did attend more regularly. But when students worked on writing assignments in class and he produced very little, he would say, "I'm such a good writer, I don't really need to do this kind of work in class." I was concerned, but my repeated attempts to talk with Ted about his writing were rebuffed. When he turned in a submission draft of his second essay, the one that asked students to use photos and texts to ultimately address what they saw as the purpose of education and literacy, I was relieved to find some potentially intriguing strands in the essay. A word, now, on how I typically commented on student work at that point (I do it a bit differently now, but I'll come back to this). Most of my comments came (and still come) in a typed memo to students at the end of their draft. In the memo, I first reflected on what I found to be the strengths of the student's work. Then, I focused on three or four primary areas to consider for portfolio revisions and/or future writing. In these primary areas, I tried to incorporate specific examples from the essay so that I showed what I meant in these comments; I also often included examples of my suggestions. Here are two paragraphs from Ted's comments that illustrate some of this:

> You seem to have found some really useful ideas in the Frederick Douglass narrative—terrific! You also seem to have developed some of your own ideas about the purpose of education and literacy, which is also really good. I think that the material you've pulled together in this essay, as well as the ideas that run through it, are a good start . . . they certainly testify to your determination, too.
>
> Now that you've got this start, I can suggest a sense of where you might go from here if you decide to revise this essay. As I say, there's a lot here to work with—that's good. The first thing we need to do is pull together what you see as the purpose for education and literacy, and make this clear in the

thesis. Right now, you begin with Frederick Douglass. That's okay, but it does make it hard for me to understand what *you* see as this purpose—and that, after all, is what the assignment asked you to write about. Throughout this essay, you seem to go back and forth between seeing literacy as power (reading gave it to him, his mistress saw him gaining power through literacy, and so on) and literacy as a way to develop peoples' minds (as a "state of grace"). I think it's possible to bring these ideas together into a thesis. For example, you could write that "The purpose of education and literacy is to help people gain power within their communities, and then to use this power to develop their own ideas and the ideas of those around them." Something like this . . . but there are a million other ways we could do this, too. We'll need to look at this together if you decide to revise the essay so that we can work on it.

In the first paragraph here, I was showing Ted where I found intriguing ideas. In the second, I was working through some issues raised in texts like Lisa Delpit's (1988) "The Silenced Dialogue," which argues that for African-American students, making codes of academic conventions explicit, and offering students ample opportunity to practice with and master those codes, is absolutely essential for their academic success. But I also was trying to leave room for Ted to develop and/or maintain control over his work. Here, I was rolling ideas about the complexities of ownership (e.g., Knoblach and Brannon, and some of my own earlier work) around in my head.[1] I didn't want to *impose* a focus on him; I didn't want him to squeeze into academic conventions, but I also realized that he needed a focus, and that his essay needed to reflect these conventions to some extent. This is reflected in the second-to-last sentence in the comments, "Something like this . . . but there are a million other ways we could do this, too." Before this sentence, my interpretation of Ted's ideas were in the foreground as I tried to suggest a structure and/or shape one he perhaps had in mind; here, I was handing the reins back to him.

In the next essay, where students investigated a question related to education and literacy, things got sticky. Ted chose to investigate what ideas high school and college writing teachers had about what students needed to be prepared for college writing. Throughout the unit, he continued to participate actively in class, but it became increasingly clear—in his contributions to discussion and small group work, and in the "low stakes" assignments leading up and contributing to the longer essay draft—that he was adrift. We worked together

---

1. But was I? When I wrote the first draft of this essay in the summer of 2001, I had just reread Delpit because I was planning a composition theory and pedagogy course. As for ownership, I've wrestled for so long with the messy connections between "helping students develop their ideas" and doing that in *school,* a place that's historically and traditionally been intended to assimilate students into the values of a dominant culture, that it suffuses every move I make in the classroom. But was I thinking about all of these at the moment I wrote these comments? I think so. But I can't really be *sure* that I was. Memory—particularly memory about something one is invested in—is hardly reliable, as Simon Schama (1991) makes so clear in *Dead Certainties (Unwarranted Speculations).*

on writing questions, gathering evidence, and doing research, but most often he would repeat, "I have this down, Mrs. Adler. Mrs. Kassner, I know what I'm doing here. I'm a great writer!" When he came to my office, he would concede to talking about his work briefly and then spend the rest of our meeting telling me that this writing *wasn't* representative, that he really had a great idea about what he was doing, that he really was a terrific writer! And when I got the submission draft of his essay, I saw that it consisted mostly of platitudes and generalities. In his self-evaluation of the essay, though, Ted wrote about how wonderful he thought the paper was, what a good job he'd done, and how strong a writer he was. I wish, in my own defense, that I still had this memo—while I remember it well, I certainly cannot quote verbatim from it the way I can from my own comments, archived (why?) on years' worth of back-up disks. Ted's letter, I think, might help to justify a response that, in retrospect, surprises me as I see my own frustration with him seeping out in unpleasant ways. I wrote:

Reading this essay—and working with you on this paper, generally—has been an interesting experience. I think it's terrific that you assert your confidence so strongly in class, and in your writing. I also have no doubt but that these strong assertions have done you pretty well in the past. The problem here is that I have a strong sense (based on my own experience) that you aren't as confident as you sound.

I want to say a couple of things here before I get to this essay. First, it is no crime to have questions about what you're doing. Sounding confident and talking a good game is great, but it isn't going to get you anywhere unless you can also *play* a good game—in this case, write a really strong essay. For instance, the self-evaluations that you write for these essays don't at all affect the way that I read them—you're not trying to convince me that the paper is great. Instead, I really want to know what you think. You may well think that you're the greatest writer since the invention of the pen, which is fine. But this self-evaluation seems to be a lot more about trying to convince me of something than it is really about what you think. Remember in our interview, when I said that I really valued thoughtfulness and thoroughness? That's what I'd really like to see in the self-evaluation and in your work in the class. And that means not always being sure that you have the answer, or that you're right—because you're thinking about things, and that's a messy process. And, back to what I said at the beginning of the paragraph, that means sometimes asking for help, which is what I'm here for (and the Writing Center is here for)!!

As for this essay, you seem to have pulled together some useful material. I really enjoyed reading the interviews that you have here. The problem for me, though, was that I wasn't at all sure what, exactly, you were investigating here. On p. 4, you write that "a lot of these students are not being prepared for college" as well as they might be—is that a point that you want to develop here? If it is, and if you revise this essay, let's work on making that clear in the beginning of the essay, and then developing strong connections between that and the material that comes after it. I have a strategy that you can use that might really help with this, but I want to sit down with you and look at this together so that I can show you how it might help.

Clearly, in the first two paragraphs I'm frustrated—with Ted generally, and especially with his use of the self-evaluation memo to convince me, yet again, of his prowess as a writer. But given Ted's comments with me about his writing, and given what I knew then from the same interviews that led me to design this class as I had, I'm not sure *why* I was frustrated or surprised. Why should I expect "genuine" responses? True, Ted was the only student who used this genre in this way—but did that mean I should fault him for it? Was I frustrated with his refusal to participate in my vision for the self-evaluation, or with his overall efforts to compensate for what I believed to be his genuine confusion and frustration? Or was I using my response to Ted as another way to communicate with him, since talking wasn't working? (Because it's now three years later, I can't say which of these I was thinking—I'd like to think the latter.) Beyond those first two paragraphs, I moved back into "helpful critic" mode, offering Ted suggestions to develop what he *had* started, and asking a question that I hoped might provide a starting place. And I told him, more directly this time, that we needed to look together at his work.

Just after I returned these comments to Ted, we also had a conference where he continued to tell me about his strong writing skills. While I tried to bring up the work that we might do on the beginnings he had (so that he could write passing final drafts for his portfolio), he kept talking about what a good writer he was. And for the first time in my teaching career, I said these words: "Ted, you're *not* that good a writer."

But even this—which I considered to be the most profoundly negative thing I'd ever said to anyone in what had then been twelve years of teaching— had no effect. He insisted that he *was,* that I would see it in his revised essays, and no, he definitely didn't need any help now, either—hadn't he not for the entire semester?

The revisions that Ted submitted in his portfolio weren't any more developed than the drafts he submitted, despite my efforts to get him to talk with me, to go to the Writing Center, to develop pieces of his writing. He didn't pass the class.

Race in Class: Stories and Lenses

The temptation now is for me to reflect on the story I've just told to arrive at a generalizable point that's meaningful for other composition instructors. Certainly, there is abundant evidence of this kind of move in composition scholarship, as we use our student stories to discuss pedagogical strategies that might have worked more effectively, or examine ideas that embody the issues raised in the stories, or any one of a number of other possibilities. Because I am working in this tradition at the same time as I am raising some gentle questions about it, I'll make that move shortly. But first, I want to play with the idea of "interpretation" to raise some additional questions through this story. To do this, I want to read the "Ted chronicle" through two lenses, considering the implications for student(s) and instructor(s) through each.

I. The Iconic Student and the Professor: Enacting Educational Myths

Through this lens, Ted's story embodies one version of an "iconic student" theme. This theme is frequently invoked in representations of students in basic writing classes, particularly in the mainstream media, but often elsewhere as well (Adler-Kassner and Harrington, 2002). The iconic student is almost always an ethnic and/or racial minority. She is portrayed as seeing education as a vehicle to gain a foothold in a culture from which she has previously been excluded. At the same time, the iconic student is portrayed by others as acted on by forces out of her control—a difficult family situation, neighborhood violence, sudden tragedy, poverty, long-term disabling circumstances. The iconic student figure is one actor in a larger narrative, the school-success narrative, which casts education as a stepping stone to participation in middle-class (dominant) culture. An essential part of participating in this narrative is both conceptualizing literacy skills as separate from any social context, so that they are not seen to reflect the interests of the dominant culture whose values they embody. These neutral skills are instead seen (by some students and some teachers) and advanced as (by the educational system, as well as institutions like mainstream media) neutral, but necessary.

Through this lens, Ted's loud proclamations of his affiliation with the school-success narrative (and its concomitant link to school-based literacy strategies, seen as necessary for participating *in* the narrative) would make his participation in it a reality. "I'm a great writer!" meant "I know what I'm doing! I'm using this system in the right way! I can do this stuff; I can overcome these circumstances!" But Ted is a victim of this myth, because his belief in it has led him to shut himself off from the possibility of working to develop literacy skills that one member of the educational system (me) has judged to be necessary for his success in that system.

Classroom Solutions Through This Lens: I. "Empowerment" through language. This solution involves a curriculum that asked students like Ted to confront the iconic student image in which this lens has him participating. The class might feature readings and assignments that channel students into identifying their own versions of the iconic student figure, then responding to that image in writing.

II. Guided assimilation. This approach would feature a curriculum that asked students like Ted to consider literacy strategies and what is *truly* necessary for college success in texts, then to build bridges between the strategies he does possess, and the ones he believes are necessary. By acquiring these strategies, it is hoped that Ted will develop a sense of his own agency within the system, and not just participate in it as an iconic student. This curriculum might feature texts with iconic students like Ted, who have made this move; writing assignments would ask Ted to find ways to use these texts as models for his own thinking, locating someone "like him" who has succeeded in the system. They might then ask Ted to extract lessons for his own education from these models, patterning his own journey through the system after these "success stories."

Comments on This Lens: In different ways, both of these solutions perpetuate the iconic student figure and the school success narrative. In both, Ted is still essentially cast as powerless within this deterministic story about schooling. These solutions also afford what I find to be a disturbing amount of power to the teacher (me), who is cast in the role of supreme insider and all-knowing being in the educational system whose job it is to guide relatively helpless, metaphorically blind students through the "labyrinth" that is that system.

I. Participating in the "Silenced Dialogue":
Confronting Race in the Classroom

This lens shifts the focus from Ted-as-victim to the interactions between me, their teacher, and this African-American student. Through this lens, I am still cast as an authority figure with power and privilege to which Ted does not have access—I am white and middle-class—but he also brings to the classroom a conceptualization of literacy, language, and education that I might not recognize, understand, participate in, condone, or choose to utilize. Ted expects different behaviors from me as a teacher than I have produced, as well as a different way of working with literacy and language education than what he is encountering in my class. These expectations are but one part of a "dialogue" that he has opened through his behaviors and his comments to me, but I have not heard his contributions correctly (or at all) and have reacted inappropriately (or, again, not at all) to them. His failure is in part a result of this silencing.

Classroom Solutions: As the teacher, I should become more educated about the different expectations that different (non-white) cultural groups hold regarding literacy conventions and literacy learning. I should also respect these students' desires to learn differently than the way I have been educated (and acculturated) to believe "all" students learn, because my ideas about "all" students really represent a dominant approach to teaching and learning writing reflected in the ideology of the process movement, which itself reflected dominant cultural ideas and values. In the specific case of Ted, I should have been more directive—more up-front with Ted about confronting the writing problems (which I, working from the culture I am from, call "issues" because I don't like the word "problems") he was clearly having with the class and talking with him even more directly about how he could work on them. I also should be more explicit about helping Ted understand the conventions suffusing academic writing as a system of codes that he must master to gain purchase in the system, and should make those codes as absolutely explicit, clear, and accessible as possible. This might be accomplished in a series of workshops on elements of those codes built into the structure of the class (e.g., "thesis," "analysis," "punctuation").

Comments on This Lens: I like this better than the iconic student/school success lens—it gives the students more agency and constructs their issues as ones that can be worked on by them and by the teacher (me). However, I think that working too strongly from a perspective that reflects Delpit's (1988) approach (in "The Silenced Dialogue," as well as in other work) is a tricky business. In a study that included interviews with students entering basic writing classes at two institutions, Susanmarie Harrington and I (2002) found that these students (regardless of race or ethnicity, class, or any other variable) believed that writing classes and writing instruction was, and would continue to be, about the development of discrete, lower-order, writing skills. On the other hand, they identified "writers" as people who communicated meaningful ideas, thoughts, and/or emotions to an audience. In other words, students didn't believe that what they were doing in writing *classes* was about *writing* at all. I worry about shifting the focus of a course so explicitly to conventions, because they can be so easily read as the *most* significant part of writing. Additionally, I strongly believe that writing classes have a "content," too—they're not just about conventions (or, for that matter, process).

The Story and Its Moral

As I said earlier, the idea of offering up a story and a moral makes me uncomfortable. I also have some serious questions about the ways that teachers represent themselves and their students in pieces like these. After all, as English (2003) suggests, the roles that teachers use to present themselves *are* just that—roles, as in a performance (see p. 119). I'm an enormously self-critical thinker and reader, so when I started to assemble Ted's story for this piece I returned repeatedly to the issue of self-construction. As I wrote, I kept returning to the request (from the editors) to "theorize" it. Theorize for what purpose? As I've tried to suggest, the "meaning" of Ted's story depends on the theoretical lens used to view it; those lenses also have implications for the ways that everyone seen through them is portrayed. I can make this a story with any number of morals, and whatever choices I make will of course reflect on me—as a teacher (because both of these students were in classes I taught), as a researcher. As Doug Hesse (2001) puts it, I can "foreground the lens, so that [the] narrated experience [becomes] the mere raw material for the stylistic ends of creating ethos" (p. 23).

Echoing a point made by Laurie Edson (2000) in the epigraph to this essay, one also made effectively by Simon Schama (1991), Hesse (2001), and others, I want to argue that the most effective thing these stories do is to show how stories serve particular purposes at particular moments. They don't reflect what happened, but they do reflect a way that I (consciously and/or unconsciously) want to portray students, myself, and my class. Quoting Hesse (2001) again, then, the significance of stories like this one "in terms of what they can do, not what they are" (p. 31).

So what can this story do? As I suggest earlier, it can draw attention to a problematic situation with a student. With the focus of my academic spotlight, it can illustrate some issues (possibilities include, but are not limited to: a student's understandings of his abilities and/or class expectations, connections between those understandings and the contexts in which they were developed, an examination of a student coming and adjusting to college and college/college writing courses). Shifting that spotlight to me, the stories can illustrate another set of issues (possibilities include, but are not limited to: benevolent racism, class structure/design, communicative strategies, teacher-student interactions). But whatever other purpose/s I chose to put this story to, it also captures the paradox that I describe earlier—it is what I choose for it to be. Ted can look like a frustrating student, or someone who's been grossly misunderstood; I can look like a frustrated, well-intentioned, competent but challenged teacher, or someone who, despite best intentions, did enormous damage to a nonmainstream student.

It's been three years now since this experience with Ted; for me, that's the equivalent of about 150 students and a change in institutions. From the experiences I've had *since* Ted, experiences undoubtedly informed *by* Ted, I can say that I do some things differently now, and with students who could be seen as far more "iconic" than Ted. I am much more up-front with students now about balancing my desire and theirs to "understand and have control over the conventions of academic writing"—from form to content to style—and leaving room for students to have power and control in the course so that they can find ways to care about their work and recognize the possibilities that writing can hold. I explain all of this to students on a letter that they receive when they walk through the door on the first day of class, even before they get a syllabus for the course. This letter also clearly (I think) spells out how I think about writing, how this is reflected in the course, and how this might be different from their previous experiences. It describes what I expect of students (to be curious, to be responsible about their work and respectful of their classmates, to complete the demanding work of the course, to be able to tolerate ambiguity and not *always* having "the answer" right away); what they can expect of me (to be supportive, to help wherever/whenever I can, to be pushy, to challenge them), and what they'll need to do to be successful in the course. Throughout the term, I give a lot of heuristic, structure-building work. When I worked with Ted, I asked students to do a lot of low-risk process writing so I could give them frequent feedback; now, I ask for even more. Much of this is in the form of "reporting" questions: "What's your question? Who's your audience? What do you know so far, and where have you learned it? What else do you need to know, and why? Where can you find this?" Questions like these make the process of knowledge-building I expect more clear, I think, and I can give clearer feedback on it.

My assignments are different, too—they now blend a focus on exploration of ideas, of process, and of genre, culminating in a multigenre essay where students use writing from different genre categories (from "newspaper and magazine writing" to "imaginative writing" to "school writing" to "visual pieces") to represent multiple perspectives on an issue. This is one way that students can explicitly explore and play with conventions, while simultaneously using those conventions in the service of the exploration and development of their own ideas. Finally, my persona in class is different—I ask students more to tell me what they think we're doing and why; I'm more directive about what needs to get done than I once was. And my comments on student work are a bit different, too. Rather than writing as an assessor of quality, as I did in the first paragraph of Ted's comments, I'm careful to write as a reader, telling students what I enjoyed, how I understood, what challenged me, what might help. I still offer three or four areas for attention, with examples from the essay and of how things might look; I still offer my ideas as possibilities. But I hope I'm clearer that these ideas come from an informed reader (in this context), not a removed, idealized judge. I also tell students when I return these drafts that the comments are meant to provide guidance, raise questions, and offer possibilities, but I'm much more clear that decisions about what to do—with their concomitant consequences, of course—ultimately lie in students' hands. Or at least, that's how I think of myself.

But is this recounting of myself any more reliable than this story of Ted and the theoretical lenses through which I could interpret it is? Am I again using particular lenses to study and report back on my own classroom behavior? Of course. And depending on the lens through which these ideas are read, my work as a teacher could seem as problematic as my recounting of Ted's behavior as a student. Aspersions could be cast on my efforts at "authenticity," and I could be seen here as trying to convince students of something that simply won't wash with them. I raise these points because I'm hesitant to use Ted's story, or any other, to come to any pithy, extractable, transferable solution. In doing so, perhaps I'm dodging the issue—and the point of this book—entirely. But I don't think so. I don't want to now leap to just the kind of conclusion I've rejected, but I do want to offer some material for additional speculation. Because our work as composition teacher-researchers is so rooted in the classroom, the scholarship we produce is almost always based on stories. Often, those stories are embedded in the research—they serve as a starting point, or as an example to be exploded, or as an idea that will be rejected. But as Edson (2000), Hesse (2001), and Schama (1991) would all have us understand, stories can be used as a lot of things that they are not necessarily, as well. When we speculate on stories, we're representing personas—and if we're included, we're one of those personas—in particular ways. Is there value in trying on these personas? Perhaps—modeling oneself after someone else, even if that someone else is oneself in a different guise—can sometimes be useful, valuable, and even validating. But pretending that these personas, these selves, these stories are *authentic* can prove problematic, as they can become part of a collection of lore that lulls us into believing that "this is the way things are." When that happens, we might stop thinking about alternatives to thinking about ourselves, our situations, the challenges we face, differently.

Works Cited

Adler-Kassner, Linda and Susanmarie Harrington. 2002. *Basic Writing as a Political Act: Public Conversations about Writing and Literacies.* Creskill, NJ: Hampton Press.

Delpit, Lisa. 1988. "The Silenced Dialogue." *Harvard Educational Review* 58 (August): 280–98.

Edson, Laurie. 2000. *Reading Relationally: Postmodern Perspectives on Literature and Art.* Ann Arbor: University of Michigan Press.

English, Hugh. 2003. "Difficulty for Whom? Teachers' Discourse About Difficult Students." In *Conflicts and Crises in the Composition Classroom,* edited by Dawn Skorczewski and Matthew Parfitt, 119–123. Portsmouth, NH: Boynton/Cook Publishers.

Hesse, Doug. 2001. "Stories, Style, and the Exploitation of Experience." *Questioning Authority: Stories Told in School,* edited by Linda Adler-Kassner and Susanmarie Harrington. Ann Arbor: University of Michigan Press.

Rose, Mike. 1989. *Lives on the Boundary.* New York: Penguin.

Schama, Simon. 1991. *Dead Certainties (Unwarranted Speculations).* New York: Alfred A. Knopf.

12

The One Who Got Away

Reflections on a Teacher's Remorse

Deborah Gussman

What if you taught a writing course and only one student failed? You might still call it a success, right? What if you taught a writing course and the student whose work you were most excited about was the only student who failed? If you were me, you might keep wondering about the one who got away.

During the 1998–99 academic year, I taught four sections of a research writing course, focusing on the Vietnam War and its impact on contemporary American society. Students worked on group presentations and individual research projects related to the topic of the Vietnam War or to the broader issues of gender, race, and nationalism that we considered. By almost any criteria, this was one of the most successful courses I had ever taught. Student evaluations of the course, across the four sections, were overwhelmingly positive—unusual for a class which is the second of two required freshman writing courses. Student performance, overall, was extremely high. Many of the final research projects were excellent: well researched and documented, thoughtfully and persuasively argued, and clearly written. In each of the classes, almost all of the students completed all of the work for the class, including a twelve- to fifteen-page research paper, with a grade of C or higher (the average final grade was a B). A few did not.

At this point, you might reasonably ask, What's the problem? Why worry about a handful of failures in a context of general success? Knowing what we know about the failure rates and difficulties associated with required writing courses across a diverse range of institutions, can the analysis of these failures be relevant? Ann Berthoff (1981) provides a possible rationale, writing that the "analysis of mistakes, misconceptions, and misstatement" is a crucial element of the development of a critical pedagogy. Min-Zhan Lu (Haswell and Lu, 2000, pp. 216, 217) suggests that stories about our failure, or "counter stories," constitute a form of "critical intervention." The implication of her argument is that writing teachers should be narrating our failures and losses, along with our successes, and locating these narratives within their institutional and material contexts since "the stories we tell (and do not tell) shape and are shaped by the material conditions of our work" Haswell and Lu, 2000, (p. 195). In a slightly different vein, Smokey Wilson (1997) asserts that any changes we make to the way we teach "must be accomplished in ways local rather than global; they must be fine-tuned not only for a particular setting but to highly specific interactive moments" (p. 11). That brings me to my "counter story" about "Stefanie," a story which describes a series of failures connected to the larger problem of defining the responsibilities of students and teachers in the writing classroom.

There wasn't anything about Stefanie that set her apart from the rest of the class. The students were all of traditional age, about evenly divided in terms of gender, and diverse racially and ethnically, as students at this university tend to be. Stefanie was about eighteen years old, easy-going, articulate, and attractive. She favored baggy athletic clothing and almost always kept her long brown hair pulled back under a baseball cap, a look that was popular with students in the 8:30 AM section. Her proposal for the research paper was what caused me to think of her as a student of promise. I had "required" students in this class to focus on a topic that mattered to them and to make a statement about their personal interest in the topic as part of their research proposal. The early results were mixed, as many of the students resisted this aspect of the assignment.

Stefanie's proposal proved to be the exception to the rule. She had decided to research the effects of the war on her hometown, a middle-class, predominately Italian-American community, near Baltimore. Her proposal was bursting with ideas, and detailed plans—to interview relatives and neighbors she knew who were veterans and anti-war protesters, to read newspaper accounts at her local library, to talk with her high school history teacher to see if he could help her to track down copies of the school newspaper from the late 1960s. She confessed that she had not taken the course because of any burning interest in the Vietnam War, but because it was a "two-fer" (it fit her need for an early morning class and got a requirement out of the way at the same time). But now, she was convinced, her research would make the war come alive by linking a remote time and situation to the places, faces, streets, and sights she knew and cared about. It seemed clear to me that Stefanie was one of a very few students who "got" what I was trying to get the class to do—to articulate a sense of ownership and investment in the research project. I wrote her an enthusiastic response, saying that I was delighted with her proposal, and eager to read more of her work.

After the proposal, though, things started to go downhill for Stefanie. Looking back, it seems to me that there are at least three possible explanations. At the time, I believed that Stefanie had failed herself. Her class attendance became erratic. She sent me an email when she first began missing classes saying she had to go home to help out with a "family situation" and that she would use the time at home to continue her research, but she never followed up with more information, and eventually, disappeared. She participated in her in-class group presentation on the anti-war movement and student protest, but her group members complained privately that she had not done her share of the preparation and had missed several meetings. Having received no draft or final paper and no word from her by the end of the term, I assumed she had dropped the course.

Then, on the last day of classes, after my final meeting with students to collect papers and do the usual "postmortem" on the course, I returned to my office. There, shoved under the door, was Stefanie's paper. It was about eight pages long, with a few parenthetical citations, no list of works cited, and no evidence of notes or a rough draft. Attached was a handwritten note, saying she had been trying to "find" me to talk about what was going on. She also mentioned that she had sent me a draft of the paper by email, and was wondering why I hadn't responded to it. Finally, she said that she knew this paper wasn't her best effort, but she hoped I'd still accept it. I sent Stefanie an email saying I'd received the paper, and would let her know something once I'd read it. After grading the final papers for the class, I wrote another email to her saying that because she'd missed so many classes, and because her final paper did not sufficiently fulfill the criteria for the assignment, I was not going to be able to give her a passing grade for the course. I also invited her to come to speak with me during my office hours that week. I never saw or heard from her again.

I suspect that most of us have had students like Stefanie, students whose promise makes us feel hopeful about our work as educators, and whose failure makes us doubt the efficacy of our strategies, or the sincerity of our endeavors. I call these feelings "teacher's remorse" to suggest the impact students have on our emotions, and the guilt and regret that come when we feel we have failed them, rather than that they have failed. This brings me to the next version of the story: the one in which I failed Stefanie. My first error was basic: I didn't communicate effectively. One limitation of electronic communication is the appearance of presence. Because Stefanie initially kept me informed via email, I had a sense of her being part of the class. Because she initiated most of the communication with me, I expected to continue to hear from her, and accepted her silence as a decision not to communicate, rather than difficulty in doing so. Did she send me a draft or try to contact me outside of class, as her note suggested? Should I have given her the benefit of the doubt? Was it right for me to discount the rest of the work she had done for the term because the final paper was unsatisfactory?

My failure to communicate is related to a second error: my uncritical investment in the idea that students are responsible for their own learning. This paradigm of student responsibility is evoked in a variety of contexts and discussions about pedagogy. I. A. Richards (1968) offered an early version of it in his model for literacy training, in which the students' role was to "explore, for themselves, their own abilities" while the teacher's role was to offer students "assisted invitations to attempt to find out what they are trying to do and how to do it" (p. 111). A variation of this theme can be found in critical literacy literature, as bell hooks' dialogue with Ron Scapp illustrates:

> The bottom-line assumption has to be that everyone in the classroom is able to act responsibly together to create a learning environment. All too often we have been trained as professors to assume students are not capable of acting responsibly, that if we don't exert control over them, then there's just going to be mayhem. (hooks, (1994, p. 152)

An increasingly popular version of this idea is the engaged learning model, described as follows:

> In engaged learning settings, students are; they take charge and are self-regulated. They define learning goals and problems that are meaningful to them; have a big picture of how specific activities relate to those goals; develop standards of excellence; and evaluate how well they have achieved their goals. They have alternative routes or strategies for attaining goals—and some strategies for correcting errors and redirecting themselves when their plans do not work. They know their own strengths and weaknesses and know how to deal with them productively and constructively. (Jones, Valdez, Nowakowski, and Rasmussen, 1995, p. 8)

The "student is responsible" paradigm is an ideal that my experience with Stefanie has caused me to question. Had I not relied so heavily on the notion that Stefanie had to be fully responsible, could I have created an opportunity for her to succeed? I have often made exceptions for students who have family problems, or are ill—why not in this case? Certainly her lack of communication at the end contributed. Yet it would not have been inappropriate for me to email or call and to give her an opportunity to explain, revise, or do make-up work. I never did that—on the grounds that her education was, in the end, her responsibility, not mine. I have become dissatisfied with that explanation. I am coming to think that it is, in part, a rationale that is supported in higher education to maintain a distance between faculty and students that serves the institution far better than the individual. I want to make it clear that I do not believe this is the intention of most individual teachers or theorists who maintain that students are responsible for their own learning—indeed, many see this position as a vehicle for liberating students from overreliance on teachers and other institutional authorities. Nevertheless, institutional policies and practices that are potentially alienating to students and faculty can result from an unexamined acceptance of this position, as my story suggests. That leads me to the third version of this story: how higher education failed both Stefanie and me.

There is a piece of the story I haven't told—the institutional and material context in which my encounter with Stefanie occurred. In 1998–99, I was teaching at the large private research university I have described here as an adjunct Assistant Professor of English on a one-year renewable contract. The small, private college at which I had worked as a tenure-track Assistant Professor for the previous five years had gone bankrupt and was taken over by this university, who dismissed the entire faculty, including myself. Thus, in being rehired by the university, I was in the position of having been "demoted" from tenure track to adjunct professor, and simultaneously "promoted" from a position in a small, little-known college to one in a large, internationally known research institution. I was teaching on two campuses. I was developing new curricula and courses while trying to find a more secure tenure-track position—an activity that involved writing papers and giving job talks, preparing writing samples, CVs and letters, traveling to institutions in several states for interviews—all of this while planning and teaching three courses per term, doing committee work, advising, the usual responsibilities of college teaching. This was being "balanced" with my family life, of course. I mention this not to complain, nor to rationalize my own actions, but to suggest that individual success and failure in the composition classroom is linked to the labor practices of institutions, the job market, the larger material world in which the "Ivory Tower" exists. In other words, Stefanie's failure was not simply the result of her individual choices and abilities, nor was it the inevitable outcome of a communication problem between an individual teacher and her student. Rather, it was related to a structural problem that affected us both. Within this structure, I had to choose where to put my time, effort, and attention. I had to choose which tasks to prioritize and which to let slide, which projects to complete and which to postpone, which students to cultivate and which to ignore.

Stefanie, as it turns out, eventually passed her required writing course. A former colleague told me recently that her second try was a success. Was that success due to a change in her life or attitude, another teacher or topic, more experience with writing? I will never know precisely what made the difference for this student. What I do know is that the problem of failure and responsibility I have described here cannot be solved by a student's individual efforts, or by the efforts of individual teachers, no matter how heroic or well-intentioned. It requires institutional change, including addressing complex issues such as workload, the use of adjuncts, job security, and the expectations of hiring institutions.

Some measures have already been taken by national organizations to address labor issues. For instance, the National Council of Teachers of English has written and published position papers such as "Statement on Class Size and Workload" (1987) and "Statement from the Conference on the Use of Part Time and Adjunct Faculty" (1997). The Modern Language Association (2002) has created committees to examine issues such as "Academic Freedom and Professional Rights and Responsibilities," "Professionalization of Ph.Ds", and "Status of Women in the Profession." Still, as Porter et al. (2000) note, while positive changes in rhetoric and composition programs have occurred as the result of administrative, classroom, and disciplinary critique, there is an ongoing need for institutional critiques that attend to "the material and spatial conditions of disciplinary practices inside a particular institution" (p. 620). They offer one optimistic model for institutional change, based on the assumption that institutions are "rhetorically constructed human designs (whose power is reinforced by buildings, laws, traditions, and knowledge-making practices) and so are changeable" (p. 611). And conceptual change is necessary if we are to imagine and to describe and to create those places which may not yet exist in higher education, in which students and teachers can do the work they need and want to do without sacrifice or remorse. As Wendy Bishop (1997) argues, we should be exploring "new attitudes and practices for learning and knowing, including: neighborliness, praxis, feminist mentoring, and the encouragement of believing behaviors" (p. 129).

Understanding my classroom problem in its larger context has also helped me to transform remorse into practical action. I have made some small but meaningful changes in my teaching practice. I now require an individual conference with students a week or two prior to their turning in the final research paper in order to review drafts and discuss their overall progress and problems. These conferences take place during class time, not in addition to it. I have also become clearer with students about my expectations. This ranges from including specific information on the syllabus such as my policy for accepting work via email, to developing a rubric for evaluating research papers and spending class time to review it. Thus, communication is now more deeply embedded in the course structure. At the same time, I am much more likely to question a student who is missing classes, and to make a phone call or send an email about missed deadlines. I now realize that one way to support the institutional status quo is to choose who or what we will sacrifice. Perhaps awareness that we are expected to make such sacrifices will make us less willing to do so routinely, and, thus, less likely to feel remorse.

Works Cited

Berthoff, Ann E. 1981. *The Making of Meaning: Metaphors, Models, and Maxims for Writing Teachers.* Upper Montclair, NJ: Boynton/Cook.

Bishop, Wendy. 1997. *Teaching Lives: Essays and Stories.* Logan, Utah: Utah State University Press.

Haswell, Richard H., and Min-Zhan Lu. 2000. *Comp Tales: An Introduction to College Composition Through Its Stories.* New York: Longman.

hooks, bell. 1994. *Teaching to Transgress: Education as the Practice of Freedom.* New York: Routledge.

Jones, Beau Fly, Gilbert Valdez, Jeri Nowakowski, and Claudette Rasmussen. 1995. *Plugging in: Choosing and Using Educational Technology.* Washington, DC: Council for Educational Development and Research, and North Central Regional Educational Laboratory. http://www.ncrel.org/sdrs/edtalk/toc.htm

Modern Language Association. 2002. "List of Committees and Commissions." (updated May 5, 2002) http://www.mla.org

National Council of Teachers of English. 1997. "Statement from the Conference on the Use of Part-Time and Adjunct Faculty." http://www.ncte.org/positions/adjunct.shtml.

———. 1987. "Statement on Class Size and Workload." http://www.ncte.org/positions/class-size-college.shtml

Porter, James E., Patricia Sullivan, Stuart Blythe, Jeffrey T. Grabill, and Libby Miles. 2000. "Institutional Critique: A Rhetorical Methodology for Change." *College Composition and Communication* 51:4: 610–42.

Richards, I. A. 1968. *Design for Escape.* New York: Harcourt.

Wilson, Smokey. 1997. "Acts of Defiance (and Other Mixed Messages): Taking Up Space in a Nontransfer Course." *Teaching English in the Two-Year College* 24: 4 (December): 13 pages. http://www.ncte.org/tetyc/back/best97.html

13

"Some People Just Don't Write Well"

Composing and Grading Amid Conflict in the Classroom

Susanmarie Harrington

"It's not fair that James doesn't get as good grades as some other people do. He just doesn't write well," Nathan said. I looked around the room at the other freshmen and sophomores in English 1302, *Advanced College Rhetoric.* Heads were nodding in agreement. I rubbed my eyes and pinched myself to make sure I was awake. Another student, Jessica, intervened, trying to be helpful: "Some people just aren't as good writers as other people are. So it's harder for them to do as well in English classes." "James works really hard," Matt said. "He should do better. It's not his fault he doesn't write well." Heads nodded some more. I don't remember what I said at that point—mostly what I remember is wishing that a fire alarm would go off so that class would have to end early. The occasion for their comments was the return of their midterm portfolios. Much to my surprise, the nine students in the class immediately shared their grades with one another. I'd never had a group of students unite in defense of a classmate like this; I'd never had a class so willing to openly discuss individual grades before. And I had no idea how to manage the convictions behind their defense of James: that grades in writing classes shouldn't be linked to writing at all.

It's not that I'd never had students who thought that effort should count, or who held the view that writing is a gift. I've had plenty of students, before and since, who arrive in class thinking that they're bad writers and nothing can be done about it (or that they're good writers, who already know everything they need to know). But this particular class was different. It was an experimental class, the first in their university to use a portfolio grading system. I was a visiting professor teaching my first undergraduate course in a new environment, and the composition program looked forward to my portfolio work. For some reason the class hadn't filled up, and at first the students and I viewed the small class size as a nice surprise. Students got more individual attention, and I had a lighter paper load. I'd have traded that paper load in a heartbeat, however, for a better psychological situation. The stress caused by the strange relationship James and I formed over the semester overshadowed everything. As the semester developed, the tension over grades spiraled out of control, affecting every aspect of class. Ironically, my other teaching assignment that semester was a graduate seminar in writing assessment. In that course, we explored the ins and outs of alternative assessments, ways of linking assessment and curriculum to further student success, and strategies for using portfolios productively. Never have I felt like such a professional fraud, as my experiences in the one class threatened to negate the claims of the other.

In 1302, the semester had started off routinely enough. I described portfolios and laid out the work for the semester. We'd be using a midterm portfolio, I explained, so that they could get a midterm grade, but nothing before that point would be graded. The weeks before midterm would allow them time to make choices, to make mistakes, to learn how to be successful. My presentation of the virtues of portfolios was rooted in ten years of experience with portfolios in a range of writing classrooms, and also in what I thought at the time was a sound theoretical footing. Like Patricia Belanoff (1994), I had long embraced the theoretical notion that "portfolios are . . . powerful instruments for change" (p. 17) and would introduce into our small class a greater option for talk and dialogue. Especially in such a small class, I anticipated that our class would be able to focus on the ways meaning is formed. As Ann Berthoff (1998) notes:

> Composing—putting things together—is a continuum, a process that continues without any sharp breaks. Making sense of the world is composing. It includes being puzzled, being mistaken, and then suddenly seeing things for what they probably are: making wrong—unproductive, unsatisfactory, incorrect, inaccurate—identification and assessment and correcting them or giving them up and getting some new ones. And all these things happen when we write: writing is like the composing we do all the time when we respond to the world, make up our minds, try to figure out things again. (pp. 3–4)

Working with portfolios in this class, I assumed that the students and I would be able to engage with composing in its richest senses. We would be able to talk about the ways in which learning to write is self-generated, creative, holistic, as well as functional and integrative of various communities and interests (here I drew on work by Jay Robinson and Patricia L. Stock, 1990). The classroom would be ripe for conversation and sense-making. The students would be able to control what work was ultimately submitted for a grade, although I did set up some structure for the portfolios. Still, they could choose from among several shorter pieces of work and several longer ones for both a midterm and final portfolio. And on every piece they submitted, they would receive feedback from me and their peers.

From the beginning, I knew that James would be a challenge. Not that he meant to be. He came to class almost every day and had his homework done.

He didn't talk too much in class but was unfailingly polite. He didn't believe he was a good writer, but he was committed to following directions. He'd read an assignment, and do just what I had asked—taking his first interpretation of the task, usually a simple interpretation, and never thinking much more about it. Where other students turned in paragraph responses to the homework, he turned in sentences. Where other students wrote two pages, he wrote half a page—always insisting, "But I did what it said to do." But he didn't always: his first assignment, a letter to me about his writing background, wasn't a letter. It covered the right content, but not in letter format. He was annoyed when I pointed this out in my response. "What difference did that make?" he asked, and turned away.

Our relationship deteriorated as the semester moved ahead. I tried to encourage James to develop his work, but he usually saw my requests for additional information or examples as criticisms. I used checklists [like those Peter Elbow (1993) suggests in "Ranking, Evaluating, Liking"] to show students the features of each essay I valued, and we talked about the checklists early in the course of working on each assignment. I tried to use them to negotiate shared values with the class. Nonetheless, James often got low rankings on his checklists, developing a love/hate relationship with them. He didn't like to read what I wrote on them, for that, to him, inevitably signaled his lack of success (even if I wrote positive comments, and pointed out places where he had great ideas worth pursuing). But he did see their value. Not unreasonably, he viewed them as signals about what I expected. Frustratingly, though, the checklists were the *only* things he looked at; he never consulted the textbook, for instance, or previous assignments, to learn how to achieve things like *arguable claim* or *appropriate evidence*. We certainly weren't engaged in a Berthoffian composing cycle, where misidentifications led to new insights. Instead, we—James and I—had cycled into frustration.

I puzzled over this cycle of frustration as I worked through some reading with my graduate students. Much of the literature on alternative assessment promotes collaboration and dialogue as fundamental components of effective teaching. I turned to scholarship for two reasons: to find out whether others had experienced such problems, and to develop generative questions that would enable me to pursue creative solutions to my problem. Work like Robinson and Stock's (1990), Elbow's (1993), and Belanoff's 1994 encourages teachers to use reflection and revision as anchors for conversations about student learning. In that theory and in my previous practice, dialogues happened. They may not have happened easily; I don't mean to suggest that simply assigning reflective pieces or portfolios changes every student's attitudes about writing. On the whole, my use of portfolios had promoted a shared understanding that ideas were developed through conversation and inquiry. But this semester in 1302, things weren't going as they should. As I read with the graduate students, I used the readings as a lens for considering the situation in the undergraduate class, and I have returned to the same readings as I have revised this story for publication.

Events took a turn for the worse when I made what would turn out to be a major mistake: I forgot to check the academic calendar before making a change in the syllabus. Because a library orientation had taken a bit longer than I'd anticipated, it ended up that midterm portfolios were due the day after midterm grades. Once I realized the error, I had to devise a way to provide midterm grades for the students before evaluating their portfolios. I did have, of course, records of the students' work, which I used to construct midterm grades, and I made a handout explaining that the grades were estimates only, based on work turned in so far. My handout said that the grades didn't really matter, and that the grade they would see on their grade report was not what would actually factor into the semester.

James was mad. I estimated a grade of C for him, and he was angry—so much so, in fact, that he and I got into an argument in the hallway that went on for close to half an hour. I could hear how counterproductive the conversation was, but I kept pursuing it, hoping that with one more turn he'd see the issues my way. (He must have felt similarly, as it was the longest conversation he ever maintained about his writing.) James remained upset, worried about how his mother would react to the C. I was upset because I didn't think the day before spring break, the day portfolios were due, was the time to be worried about grades. The portfolio was done. And on top of that, James had never wanted to do anything about his performance. From the start, he had resisted my entreaties that he conference with me. "Is all my work turned in?" he would ask. "Yes," I would say, for James was always up on his work. "Then I don't need a conference. If I want to see what you like, all I need to do is look at the handout." No matter how many times I urged him to come see me, to visit the Writing Center, to revise, he refused. He did what he did—he did what I wanted, as far as he was concerned—and he got a C. My pointing out that his revisions were what mattered simply went over his head. He left mad and shared his feelings with Matt and some other classmates in the dorm.

I found myself turning to a pair of essays from my graduate course: a critique of Peter Elbow's work by Michael Bernard-Donals (1998), and an epistolary essay by Bernard-Donals and Elbow (1998) entitled simply "Differences of Opinion." In the graduate class, we read these essays as examples of inquiry; I turned to them privately hoping to gain some insight into how assessment systems play out for better and worse in particular classrooms. Bernard-Donals (1998), a former student of Elbow's, positions himself at the start of his own essay: "I was one of Elbow's students . . . and so I began as quite sympathetic to his pedagogies. Over the year I have grown more and more skeptical of some of the assumptions that guide Elbow's work, but have found nevertheless that what he says more often than not *works*" (p. 53). But Bernard-Donals argues in the end that open-ended evaluation (like the checksheets I was using) "seems to work pretty much like ranking or grading. If ranking and grading establishes a set of norms . . . evaluation—in which writing is seen as bound to the contexts of its production—replaces it with another foundation: classroom consensus"

(p. 60). Bernard-Donals focuses his attention on the content of students' essays and the ways classroom consensus affects students' choices. In my classroom, content negotiations were not the issue. Rather, writing evaluation became tied to the perceived effort put forth for students' essays, and a pitched battle between students' consensus and my approach ensued. The student consensus about the nature of grading formed a solid foundation for them. Additionally, James simply resisted the open-ended evaluation. One assumption in Elbow's pedagogy is that students will read the teacher's open commentary. I'm not sure James ever read anything I wrote beyond the places I checked on the continuum. He converted the "yea to boo" continuum into a grading scale, and he didn't like where he stood.

As it turned out, James actually got a C+ on his midterm portfolio, but the slight improvement didn't matter to him. He continued to resist revising. He continued to read the handouts and checklists carefully, but he never believed that the criteria on them were anything but my inventions. One of his self-assessments said, "I think all my microthemes are good but I am afraid that when I submit them to you they won't get a good grade, maybe because you won't like them." He never responded to my questions about how he knew they were good, or whether what he thought was good might (or might not) be the same as what I thought was good. Where did we each get those criteria? I was fascinated by this question (which was, after all, motivating my graduate seminar); James wouldn't acknowledge it. He stopped coming to class quite so regularly, although he basically kept up on things. Whenever he missed, he had Matt to talk with back in the dorm.

The midterm argument spilled over into the rest of the class, and the atmosphere changed. I'd been expecting that; the grades were like a big bend in the road of the semester; once we were around it, the landscape looked different. There was still plenty of time for grades to move (up or down) before the semester ended, but a grade was on the table. And the students rebelled, rallying around James. The situation was complex. James' insistence that he was doing what I wanted, and the class' willingness to value effort over all else collided with my view that they could learn the fundamentals of argument. Their conviction that writing talent was born, not made, grew stronger. Individually and collectively, they defended James for trying and criticized me for not giving him enough credit. I remembered one of Peter Elbow's letters (in his exchange with Bernard-Donals) focusing on issues of pressure and stress: "Students can deal better with tricky pressure and constraints if they have a clearer and more vivid sense of *what they themselves think and want;* . . . they can figure this out better in situations of lower pressure and danger; . . . they often get bamboozled about what they think and want when they always operate under conditions of maximum pressure and danger" (1998, p. 73). My problem, I realized, was that I couldn't get James to consider *what he thought and wanted.* His entire attention was focused on what (he thought) *I* wanted, and his classmates' attention was focused on my supposed failure to appreciate that James was working hard. The upshot was more pressure and danger for all of us. The students weren't writing to make sense of the world, as Berthoff would have it; they were writing to make sense of my expectations.

What made the situation virtually unbearable for me was that the class's defense of James was rooted in two fundamental misconceptions: one, that he was putting forth real effort, and two, that his grade was the lowest in the class. They thought Matt's grades were higher than James', even though James was working much harder. This claim undermined the legitimacy of the grades still further. Trouble is, this wasn't true: Matt's grade at midterm, and his performance overall, was generally a half to full letter grade below James'. I couldn't tell the students what I thought about either of these things without breaching confidentiality. I could only point to the course goals, the textbook, and the criteria listed for each assignment sheet and say, "No, effort isn't what counts. Your achievement in all these areas counts. And believe me, you can learn this. That's why we have a course."

James continued to submit technically complete, conceptually vague work, and at the end of the semester, he fell just short of the number of points needed to get a C. I rounded his grade up, figuring that the weird dynamics of the semester had been as much my doing as his, and that he probably understood the situation even less than I did. And so I ensured that he passed the class with the grade he needed to move on to other requirements.

What have I learned? Several things—most importantly, that some moments in teaching are inscrutable. I don't really understand what made this class circle around James this way, or why it was that portfolio grading caused this group so much trouble. In part, I wonder whether my years away from a campus with dormitories made me lose some touch with how residential campus student culture operates. My calendar error had big repercussions. But that doesn't explain everything that happened. I knew the assessment issues involved in introducing portfolios, after all, I had worked successfully with other undergraduate classes, I had thought carefully about challenges like those raised by Nick Carbone and Margaret Daisley (1998) about grades as rhetorical symbols, and I had years of experience teaching with portfolios, having guided students through reflection, selection, evaluation, and presentation. Perhaps it was the unique combination of personalities that shaped our relationships. James said that his English teachers "always gave Cs." And that's what he got in my class, too. He came in expecting another English teacher to give him a C, and that's exactly what happened.

I don't want to place all the blame on James. After all, I was the one in authority, and I am the one with the broader context for this particular class dynamic. And I do know now that James was right about one thing: paper grades do matter. His mother saw his C, and never his "real" midterm portfolio grade. The two grades weren't much different, but James did have a point: grades are real, and when they appear on a midterm transcript they have power. I was wrong to have muffed the dates in the first place, and I was more wrong to have told the students those grades didn't matter. They are powerful symbols, and saying they aren't doesn't alter that fact. Carbone and Daisley (1998) argue that it is possible

> to conclude the course in agreement with our students that their grades repre-
> sent not so much a terminal judgment (although outsiders may read it as
> such), but a sign that recalls specific and useful memories about their writing,
> and which guides them on the road to further learning. (p. 92)

I've realized that the entire structure of the semester must be organized around creating such "specific and useful memories." A portfolio is, in that sense, a scrapbook whose artifacts prompt teacher and student alike to generate those memories. For James, there was no memory in the class; every interaction with me was simply an enactment of the "yea/boo" continuum. Thankfully, such a problem hasn't occurred since, and I like to think that this is in part because I'm actively building additional reflection into the class and responding more to students' reflective work, especially earlier in the semester. This creates more of the discursive space Elbow (1993) advocates, and it helps encourage us to focus on the memories of learning that has happened, seeing possibilities for learning yet to come. It focuses collective attention on making sense of the world and of controversial public issues; it encourages each member of the class to develop a greater sense of what she or he thinks and wants.

Could I have intervened earlier in the semester to redirect the class's reaction to James? In subsequent classes, I've not had such a small group, so the chances of a similar dynamic occurring have been lessened. But I've tried to anticipate such dynamics, and head them off, with more coordinated presentations of grading rubrics, checklists, and textbooks. Showing students—especially in a multisection course—how what we're doing feeds into a larger structure is one part of this coordination; another is getting them involved in reading sample essays and generating criteria. This involves all of us in assessment throughout the term, and it focuses attention on how teacher criteria develop in the context of the program and department expectations. James's class never bought into the curriculum's criteria for assignments, and they couldn't see that my criteria had roots in their local context.

In the end, I recognize the presence of what I think of as "The James Factor" in my classes. Some students do try hard, without much success. They need to know that their trying is valued. This isn't to say that I grade much on effort. I don't. I have restructured how I think about class preparation time and have become much more intentional about classroom time. I build in reflections on class participation, and I give out guidelines for participation that encourage students to see that a range of behaviors—from talking in class to listening well to functioning in small groups to asking questions—combine to create effective participation. Perhaps James's frustration grew from his lack of awareness about his effort: he couldn't focus his effort in ways that fully matched the course requirements, and I may not have helped him see how our sequences of activities led towards our assignments. I make it more my job now to guide students' effort, to reward them for it, and to promote conversations that help students bridge the gaps between effort and outcome.

This is an ongoing challenge. While I firmly believe that every student can learn more about writing in the course of a semester, I see more clearly now that students who enter our courses believing themselves to be poor writers who can't change that fact do have additional challenges to face. Their previous socialization comes into the classroom with them. As I conclude this essay, I'm drawn back into the challenge that Russel Durst (1999) outlines in *Collision Course: Conflict, Negotiation, and Learning in College Composition.* While Durst is explicitly concerned with political conflicts in the classroom, he also worries that we reject students' perceptions of what they need. As he notes, "we set up our classes by asking students to critique and resist authority; we just don't want them to question *our* authority as we ignore or dismiss their own goals" (p. 176). My class vigorously questioned my authority; they resisted my notion that grades should reward outcome, not effort. They had their own goals for the semester, and I failed to take those goals seriously. In retrospect, what I would do, had I the chance, is listen harder to that argument. I would have found ways to bring that argument into class—perhaps by drawing together some readings about grading and offering them to the class to analyze. In that way, our academic analysis of argument would have continued and our debate about grading would have been more profitable. The resulting atmosphere might have been more welcoming for James, who might have found his views situated a little differently. How to make all our classrooms welcoming space for student like James, who come to our classes believing they cannot succeed, is a challenge worth pursuing.

Thanks to the students of English 5365 (Spring 1999), whose conversations about writing assessment helped me think about my teaching as this story happened, and to Linda Adler-Kassner, who helped me think about it both in the moment and in the writing of it.

Works Cited

Belanoff, Patricia. 1994. "Portfolios and Literacy: Why?" *New Directions in Portfolio Assessment.* Eds. Laurel Black, Donald A. Daiker, Jeffrey Sommers and Gail Stygall. Portsmouth, NH: Boynton/Cook Publishers. 13–24.

Berthoff, Ann, with James Stephens. 1998. *Forming/Thinking/Writing,* 2nd ed. Portsmouth NH: Heinemann Boynton/Cook.

Bernard-Donals, Michael. 1998. "Peter Elbow and the Cynical Subject." In *The Theory and Practice of Grading Writing: Problems and Possibilities,* edited by Frances Zak and Christopher C. Weaver, 53–66. Albany NY: SUNY Press.

Carbone, Nick, and Margaret Daisley. 1998. "Grading as a Rhetorical Construct." In *The Theory and Practice of Grading Writing: Problems and Possibilities,* edited by Frances Zak and Christopher C. Weaver, 77–94. Albany NY: SUNY Press.

Durst, Russel. *Collision Course: Conflict, Negotiation, and Learning in College Composition.* City: Publisher. Urbana IL: NCTE, 1999.

Elbow, Peter. 1993. "Ranking, Evaluating, and Liking: Sorting Out Three Forms of Judgment." *College English* 55.2:187–206.

———— and Michael Bernard-Donals. 1998. "Differences of Opinion: An Exchange of Views." In *The Theory and Practice of Grading Writing: Problems and Possibilities,* edited by Frances Zak and Christopher C. Weaver, 67–74. Albany NY: SUNY Press.

Robinson, Jay L. and Patricia L. Stock. 1990. "Literacy as Conversation: Classroom Talk as Text Building." In *Conversations on the Written Word: Essays on Language and Literacy,* edited by Jay Robinson. Portsmouth, NH: Boynton/Cook Heinemann.

14

How Not to Lead a Class Discussion

Dawn Skorczewski

"They wouldn't answer my question." "They looked at me like I had just spoken another language." "I don't think they read the assigned text." "It was like pulling teeth." We've all taught classes in which the discussion simply does not work. When we try to describe what happens in these hours, we often use visceral images that depict us as dentists pulling teeth from patients who have not been given anesthetic, or as miracle workers raising bodies from the dead. We cast ourselves as hardworking professionals who face crowds of lazy or passive or baffled students. When the discussion is not working, we invoke our authority and expertise as teachers to think carefully about what to do. But when our discussions go well, we are more likely to use plural pronouns and emotive imagery to talk about them. We say that "we were in the groove," "on the same wavelength," or "tuned in." When it goes well, in other words, we relax into it; we let it flow. We become an earnest group of human beings thinking and arguing together. But what are we doing when the discussion is at its best? How is it that a teacher uses his or her expertise to transform a mass of individuals into a community of thinkers on any given day? In short, what does a teacher do to make the discussion work?

Consider this comment, from an award-winning teacher at an institution that enrolls students with very high grades and SAT scores: "When they are not talking, and I have tried every kind of question I know, I simply throw up my hands and lecture; this can go on for a semester. So I just chalk up the bad classes to experience and wait for the next good one to come along." For this teacher, there is nothing to be done about students who do not answer her pointed textual questions. When her usual moves do not work, the class enters a stalemate, which she ends by becoming the only speaker in the room. We might argue that this teacher presents a simple problem, and that she needs discussion-leading strategies to help her "save" the bad class. I might agree, except that when I have offered teachers I supervise a set of suggestions such as those from teaching manuals (see Brookfield and Preskill, 1999; Gottschalks, 1994; and Tiberius and Tipping, 2000), the teachers often found that their discussions still lacked energy and direction. I have also tried those techniques myself, with very mixed results. These experiences have led me to believe that perhaps more than a set of discussion-leading skills, teachers who want to improve their class discussions need ways of thinking about what is happening in their classrooms that are more specific to them, the language, or grammar, in other words, of their particular classrooms.

How does one speak about a teacher's "felt sense" of what it means to lead a classroom? I believe that we might begin to answer this question by examining moment-to-moment interactions between students and teachers in discussions that go awry. When teachers monitor their own and their students' reactions in the "here and now" of a discussion, they can first identify, and then make explicit use of their ways of interacting with students in the classroom as clues to improving their pedagogy.

As we lead discussions, we monitor the discussion with what Theodore Reik (1948), drawing from Freud's concept of "evenly hovering attention," calls "a third ear." We are both in the discussion and we are watching it from outside, looking for signs of students' interest, disinterest, engagement, or boredom. We monitor the conversation even as we participate in it. We help it stay on course, but we also look for cues about its direction. Henry Smith explains that "Evenly-hovering attention . . . serve[s] a kind of gyroscopic function in allowing the [teacher] to be both fixed and free, to scan for what may be missing, to return to a point at centre, and to be alert for surprises from multiple directions" (Smith, 1995, p. 69). Like the analyst, in other words, the teacher cultivates the ability to "listen simultaneously on many levels" (Heimann, 1950, p. 82). We might say that this happens all the time in discussions in writing classrooms, that we monitor the discussions we are leading from within and from the outside. We pay attention to our students' and our own reactions, even those just outside the realm of our immediate attention, as we attempt to keep ourselves and the class on track.

One of the requirements of my first semester writing course is that students lead a twenty-minute discussion of one of the readings on our syllabus. On the first day of class, I distribute a sign-up sheet and a list of suggestions for how to lead a discussion. I also include a list of the criteria by which the students will be judged: imagination, engagement with the text, and authoritative management of the conversation, student-centered writing activities, and enthusiasm. When we consider the discussion as something a class is creating together, something that is both in and outside of the individuals in the room, we monitor our own experiences of "it" for clues for how and where to proceed. We note our tension when a student who talks all the time raises her hand yet again, for example, or the anger that rises up in us when a student opens his mouth and releases an audible yawn. But what do we do once we have identified these reactions? And how do we teach new instructors to pay attention and act on their own reactions without becoming paranoid—reactive to every single gesture students make in a classroom?

Halfway through the semester in my graduate course in teaching composition last year, we confronted this dilemma head on. Sharon was leading a discussion of Mary Louise Pratt's (2002) "Arts of the Contact Zone." She began by asking a string of "guess what I am thinking and I will tell you if you are right" questions. "What is the contact zone?" she asked. "Where does Pratt talk about literacy?" "What is autoethnography?" The usually boisterous class became silent. A few students attempted to answer, but Sharon was unable to channel their answers into a larger discussion. Once they had defined the terms she listed, she did not have an idea of what they should do. She seemed frozen, responded in a monotone, with few words, and moved to present another series of questions. After each question a silence descended on the room. Quickly, the silence was filled by another question.

Sensing what I thought was a look of desperation on Sharon's face, and frustration on the faces of her students, and attending as well to my own feelings of anxiety and helplessness, I asked Sharon if we could call a "freeze frame" to discuss our progress thus far. Sharon nodded. Several students said that they felt that she had an idea of what they should say, and so they felt hesitant to speak. I concurred, adding that perhaps they could assist Sharon in finding a way to ask more open-ended questions. As I finished speaking, I noticed that Sharon had begun to cry. Other students noticed too. I felt the eyes of the class on me, and I struggled internally with what to do. Was this my fault? Had I precipitated a discussion that might have evolved more naturally, or at the very least, been initiated by Sharon rather than me?

"Oh dear," I said, "I am sorry if this freeze frame upset you."

"It's not you," she said, "or anyone here." "I have PMS. I always cry when I have PMS." Many of the students laughed. One woman said, "I know exactly what you mean." Another woman commented that Sharon was brave to be so forthright in front of the class. In the minute that followed, Sharon regained her composure, asked another, more open-ended question, and proceeded to manage a discussion that became quite lively. It was particularly enhanced by the comments of the women in the room, who began to take charge of the movement of the discussion. They provided examples from their own lives, made connections between quotations from the text and their experiences, and referred to each other's comments when they spoke. One woman brought up a text the students had read for the previous class, an essay by Adrienne Rich (2002), "When We Dead Awaken: Writing as Re-Vision." She thought that the poems in Rich's essay were examples of writing from the contact zone, but she was not a big fan of the essay overall. She felt (as students often do when they read this essay) that Rich's tone was too dogmatic.

I relaxed in my chair as this discussion proceeded. Sharon was in control, and her classmates were helping her. They had become a working group, and they appeared to be enjoying themselves as well. Sharon's PMS comment had, I believed, altered the implicit relationships in the classroom by calling attention to the fact that they were all human beings, trying to do their best in sometimes-challenging circumstances. As I smiled to myself, one of the men in the class, Kevin, joined the conversation in an animated way. He agreed that Rich was dogmatic. He said that he was particularly angry with Rich's use of Diane Wakowski's poetry as an example of feminist writing. Rich's characterization of Wakowski was, he argued, completely wrong. He provided evidence. "I know Diane Wakowski. I had dinner with her one night when she read in Oakland, California, where I was a student before I transferred here. The poet Rich describes is nothing like the Diane Wakowski I know. Diane Wakowski is a wonderful lady."

As Kevin spoke, I continued to feel content with the way the class was moving. The students were engaged in a real discussion; they were making connections between the text and their lives, and had even ventured into another text for evidence for the debate. The student discussion leader had been saved, and might even decide that she had led a wonderful discussion after all. Buoyed by my relief, I then made a terrible mistake. I laughed aloud at Kevin's comment about Wakowski. I kept thinking about the presidential debate in which one candidate turned to the other and said, "Senator, you are no Jack Kennedy." As I laughed, others in the room joined me. After a moment, the room had dissolved into giggles and chuckles.

Kevin, however, was not laughing. He looked at me quizzically. "What are you laughing about?" I told him what his comment had reminded me of. The class looked at me, puzzled. Not one of them had heard this before. Second, they reacted to Kevin's face. He was hurt.

Suddenly I realized that my laughter emanated more from relief than from recognition of an old memory. I had been so nervous about Sharon's discussion, particularly my interruption of it that I had seized on Kevin's example as a ready release. In the process, I made him into an escape valve for the anxious energy that had gathered in the room, and in me. The class had joined me, perhaps because they too were on edge, and because I was giving them permission to laugh at this moment, just as I had given them permission to try to assist Sharon when I called a freeze frame. I also suspected that Kevin's gender contributed to my laughter. Was it possible that I was slightly embarrassed that women's bodies had entered our discussion? Perhaps I felt the need to assert my authority in response to a man, to show that women teachers could be "in charge" without having to deny that they also have bodies? At each of these moments, I held the authority in the room about as stridently as a teacher can; I authorized laughter in Kevin's case, and criticism of another student, in Sharon's. And my feelings of anxiety, embarrassment, and relief became the group's to manage rather than simply my own.

I realized the irony of my wielding of teacherly authority in a freeze frame attempt to "save" someone else's discussion in the split second that I saw Kevin's hurt face and noted the faces of his classmates, who clearly sympathized with him. So I decided that I needed to apologize to Kevin and called another freeze frame. This time I would be the one whose pedagogy was up for discussion, I said, and I encouraged all of the students to comment on my disruption of the discussion. I purposely invited criticism at this point. I told my students that criticizing the instructor is very hard for students to do, that I recognized that it was difficult but that I really thought I had hurt someone's feelings, and I wanted them to comment on how this had happened, if they could. In the back of my mind I realized that this conversation could lead us right back to our discussion of the contact zone. But I also recognized that I was taking control of the class again—Sharon had no authority in this situation except as the discussion leader.

The tension in the room as I called a freeze frame to discuss my laughter at Kevin was palpable. Several of the women who had come to Sharon's rescue said that they thought my laughter had hurt Kevin's feelings and disrupted the class. Kevin insisted that he was merely confused, but I feared he could not say that he'd been hurt as well. I suggested that the problem was the way I was using my authority as a teacher even though it was not mine to use at that moment in the discussion, since another student was actually in that role. I was introducing a "way of being together" with my students that did not correctly fit the situation. In other words, I was misreading their implicit cues about how they wanted to be taught. Many students agreed. Susan, a student who could always be counted on to say exactly what was on her mind, suggested that we correct the problem by returning the leadership of the discussion to its rightful owner. All agreed, and the contact zone debate ensued once again. My comment and the freeze frame after it were not attended to again.

This example of what might be called an "interactive error" offered opportunities for me and my students to discover and explore "new ways of being together" in the classroom, ways that expanded our understanding of each other, the course material, and what was possible for us to do in the classroom (Tronick 2003, p. 2). It also taught me something about how important it is to consider when to reveal observations made by my "evenly hovering attention" in the classroom. When I called a freeze frame in Sharon's discussion, my internal reactions to the discussion were not terribly productive when shared with my students, because I was not the one in charge. In addition, my attention was not really "even"; my students' positions in the conversation were not taken into account, and my effort "to help" backfired into a usurpation of two students' authority. Add to this the difficult issue of the emotional atmosphere in the classroom when the conversation is stilted or when most of the class sits in silence while a few students attempt to move the conversation along. It would seem to be a wonderful strategy to attempt to release anxiety in such a class. But to do so at the expense of one of the students is neither fair nor productive, particularly when the anxiety is also, clearly, my own.

Perhaps the most valuable lesson to be learned from this and the other teaching encounters I have described here is of one of humility and flexibility. If a teacher can listen carefully to what is happening in the classroom, and respond to what is happening there from moment to moment, she might well be able to attend to and continue to shape what is going on even as she invites the

class to have a say in what that is. A class is something that students and teachers create together, so it is not the sole domain of the instructor to ensure that
the discussion works. But it is the instructor's role to set up the conditions under which discussions might thrive, to closely monitor her reactions to the discussion as it is taking place, to try to see what she is bringing to the conversation, and to make the classroom a place where discussion of the here and now
is a natural thing to do. In this sense, the teacher has a role in helping students
establish and explore the parameters of what is possible to be thought and said
in the classroom. This is particularly the work of an instructor in the very first
part of a course, when a teacher demonstrates his or her willingness to, as
Rouzie (2001) terms it "engage in the play" (p. 287).

My own favorite metaphor for the classroom discussion originated from
early conversations about the teacher's "bag of tricks." Rather than thinking of
the classroom as a place in which we perform tricks, or teach our students to do
so, I now tend to imagine the classroom as a space we enter with our own "bags
of toys." Our bags of toys are special to us, even precious, and they have been
with us for so long that we sometimes take it for granted that they exist at all.
Call these toys experiences. They may be interpersonal, as in our ways of relating in a group: lively or thoughtful, strident or shy. They may include our
personal tastes and opinions, such as how we like the chairs to be close to each
other in the circle, without extra ones in the middle, or how we like the break
to occur two-thirds of the way through the class rather than halfway (so the last
part flies by). They may include our ways of reading, with a pen, or highlighter,
and our preference for reading aloud in a slow, thoughtful voice. They may also
include our ways of questioning: in the voice of a pensive philosopher, or a
drill sergeant, or a talk show host, or a crafty artisan.

If we are to have successful classes, we must attend to the fact that our students come into the classroom with their own bags of toys, most of which include the offerings of their previous teachers as well as those of parents, peers,
and all of the other important relationships and experiences they have had.
Whatever we all hold in our bags, it can be the case in any classroom that some
peoples' toys matter much more than others. I recall a classroom, for example,
in which our instructor effectively walked into the room, dumped her toys on
the desk, built a beautiful interpretation with them, and then invited us to do the
same. Or how about the classroom in which the only toys that matter are students' experiences? Course evaluations of such classrooms often indicate that
the students wanted more guidance from the instructor. In the classroom discussion that I am trying to imagine here, students and teacher enter the room,
spread their toys out on the floor, and then experiment with and think about
what they might create together. They also reflect on what they are doing as
they construct it, both to name what they are doing for themselves and to de-
termine where they will go in their future work together. It is together, then,
that they shape what is called discussion, and this discussion changes shape as
it goes.

Works Cited

Bartholomae, David and Anthony Petrosky. 2002. *Ways of Reading: An Anthology for Writers,* 6th edition. Boston: Bedford St. Martin's.

Brookfield, Stephen and Stephen Preskill. 1999. Discussion as a Way of Teaching. San Francisco: Jossey-Bass.

Gottschalks, Katherine. 1994. *Facilitating Discussion: A Brief Guide.* Ithaca, NY: Cornell University Press.

Heimann, Paula. 1950. "On Countertransference." *International Journal of Psychology* 31: 81–4.

Pratt, Mary Louise. 2002. "Arts of the Contact Zone." In *Ways of Reading: An Anthology for Writers,* 6th edition, edited by David Bartholomae and Anthony Petrosky, 605–26. Boston: Bedford St. Martin's.

Reik, Theodore. 1948. *Listening with a Third Ear: The Inner Experience of a Psychoanalysis.* New York: Farrar Strauss & Co.

Rich, Adrienne. 2002. "When We Dead Awaken: Writing as Re-Vision." In *Ways of Reading: An Anthology for Writers,* 6th edition, edited by David Bartholomae and Anthony Petrosky, 627–52. Boston: Bedford–St. Martin's.

Rouzie, Albert. 2001. "Conversation and Carrying-on: Play, Conflict, and Serio-Ludic Discourse in Computer Conferencing." *College Composition and Communication* 53: 251–99.

Smith, Henry.1995. "Analytic Listening and the Experience of Surprise." *International Journal of Psychoanalysis* 76: 67–78.

Tiberius, Richard. 1989. *Small Group Teaching: A Trouble-Shooting Guide.* Monograph Series/22 OISE Press/The Ontario Studies in Education.

Tiberius, Richard and J. Tipping. 2000. "The Discussion Leader: Fostering Student Learning in Groups." In *Teaching Alone, Teaching Together: Transforming the Structure of Teams for Teaching,* edited by J. L. Bess and Associates, 108–30. San Francisco: Jossey-Bass.

Tronick, E. Z. Forthcoming, "Of Course All Relationships Are Unique." *Psychoanalytic Inquiry,* v 23, n 3, 2003.

15

Teaching Without Armor

Eric V. Martin

After completing my doctorate in English at Illinois State University in 1995 and working there for a year as the Assistant Director of Writing Programs (a full-time, non-tenure track appointment), I accepted my first tenure-line position at The University of Findlay—a small, private school of approximately 4,000 students in Findlay, Ohio. Early in my academic career, I taught three sections of a basic writing course. Like many such courses, the freshman writing course was designed to capitalize on students' experiences and then guide them to argumentative discourse. The same course at Illinois State focused on persuasive and analytical writing from the outset, although it did include a personal essay assignment. Most ISU students stayed on safe terrain when writing that essay. They typically wrote about either winning/losing the big game in high school or coping with the death of a grandparent. Few students at ISU took greater risks in that particular paper, and few instructors considered the possibility of pressing students beyond superficial recountings of events. In other words, personal information was shared, but only in truncated and predictable ways. Thus, when I first learned that the freshman writing course at Findlay focused on personal writing, I anticipated reading many more "safe" essays. I imagined that I would be covering familiar terrain, but I could not have been more wrong.

Of course, I knew going in that things would be somewhat different at Findlay—a school five times smaller than my alma mater. Although I had never attended a small college myself, I understood that the small college experience is defined by small classes, regular contact with professors who are dedicated to teaching and advising, and an overall concern for the individual student's welfare and success. However, I could never have anticipated the lengths to which such an institution will go in order to accommodate students, and how such concern for the individual student would affect my role as a teacher. The case of Helen W. begins to illustrate what I mean.

Helen was a freshman enrolled in my course. She was a double major (Pre-Veterinary Medicine and Equestrian Studies), and based on her early work in my course, she appeared to be a promising writer. Unfortunately, she was also a very troubled young woman and class attendance soon became a problem. The following three memos aptly demonstrate my point above.

MEMORANDUM 1

Week 8 of the semester

To: Eric Martin

From: Director of Counseling Services

Re: Your Student, Helen W.

> This is to inform you that Helen W. has been seen at the Counseling Services for symptoms related to depression. Those symptoms include insomnia, pervasive sadness, withdrawal and isolation, anxiousness, and inability to concentrate. These are likely affecting her attendance and/or performance in her classes. Please do not hesitate to call if you have any questions or concerns.

MEMORANDUM 2

Week 9 of the semester

To: Eric Martin

From: Vice President for Academic Affairs

Re: Your Student, Helen W.

> The Director of Counseling Services has notified this office that Helen W. will miss some classes this week due to coping with the loss of her horse. Please work with Helen as she struggles to work through this crisis in her life.

> > [Note: Equestrian Studies majors at Findlay are able to board their horses at University farms located several miles south of the main campus. Helen's horse died unexpectedly during her first semester on campus.]

MEMORANDUM 3

Week 16 of the semester

To: Eric Martin

From: Chair, Academic Standards Committee

Re: Your Student, Helen W.

Recently you indicated to the Director of Counseling Services that you plan to fail Helen W. in your course because of excessive absences (13). I am writing to inform you that Ms. W has since appealed to this committee for a late withdrawal from your course. Attached you will find letters of support from the Director of Counseling Services as well as Ms. W.'s psychologist. These explain Ms. W.'s battle with depression—a battle which began when she was sexually abused as a child and which resulted in a suicide attempt not long ago. Due to recent changes in her medication as well as several circumstances beyond her control (including the death of her horse), this committee is inclined to support her request. Please let us know if you have additional information that we should consider.

As I received these memos, I could not help but be amazed as faculty members, staff members, and administrators went out of their way to assist this student. Undoubtedly, she would not have received such gentle treatment at most larger schools. During my time at Illinois State, for example, I had numerous students who missed seven, eight, and more class meetings. These students simply failed the course. I neither saw nor heard from most again. On those few occasions when students did try to plead a case in an effort to wiggle around the attendance policy, I did everything but close my eyes, stick my fingers in my ears, and sing "It's the Hard-Knock Life." Like most instructors at larger schools, I was not encouraged to know or even be especially interested in knowing my students beyond their work for my classes. And while I did not always feel comfortable with this practice, I wore my armor well.

At Findlay, the barrage of memos and phone calls hit immediately and never quit. Like most work places, personal information was exchanged around office coffeepots, and it thrived in the campus snackbar. At Findlay it also sprang from my mailbox each morning in the form of memos like those above, it throbbed in the red light of my phone's message button, and it downloaded itself into my computer throughout the day. This culture of personal contact was reinforced and extended in writing courses. After making one assignment that asked students to discuss a significant person (or people) in their lives, I received essays describing what it is like to be the child of an alcoholic, essays explaining life in a gang and the problems with leaving that life behind, and essays sharing ongoing struggles with eating disorders. I even received an essay in which a student discussed her grandmother as the most significant person in her life—not because her grandma's house was cozy in the winter and smelled of freshly baked cookies, but because grandma was named this student's guardian when her father was sent to prison for killing her mother.

Although I am certain that witnessing a parent's murder is not an everyday experience for most college students on campuses of any size, I am equally certain that issues such as alcoholism, drug abuse, gang violence, and eating disorders impact many more students than we realize. Such experiences are not unique to students at The University of Findlay. My students at Illinois State undoubtedly had many such experiences themselves, but most of those students never revealed as much when completing a similar assignment. The setting simply did not encourage disclosure even when the possibility was raised (albeit limitedly) with a personal essay assignment. At that school, like most others of its size, invitations to share deeply personal information were nonexistent; at Findlay, such invitations seemed to spring from every corridor, which made disclosure eminent. I had not anticipated the intensity of this difference when I started at Findlay, but it soon became clear in my course as well as in my day-to-day interactions with colleagues and supervisors.

At first the students' tendency to reveal profoundly personal information made me uncomfortable, and the administration's earnestness in responding to nearly every student setback frustrated me. However, during my three years at Findlay, I came to value the more personal climate. My teaching changed for the better because my priorities shifted. When I started teaching freshman composition in 1990 at a school enrolling over 20,000 students, *I* selected the topics and the readings, and my students wrote in response to assignments that *I* devised. Back then, I wanted to know that every course reading and important rhetorical concept was covered and that nearly every scrap of student text exhibited the features of traditional academic discourse. I certainly was not opposed to assigning personal narratives or even getting to know my students personally. However, these were add-ons. Coverage of the more "academic" matters was my first priority, and there simply was not much time for lengthy personal exchanges. I was a fine teacher by all accounts, but I was not a complete teacher.

After teaching for three years at a much smaller school, I now find myself wanting to explore with students those topics which truly engage them instead of just me. I want their work to grow out of their questions, their trials, and their tribulations even if it means that certain things about "academic writing" go uncovered and certain student revelations make me uncomfortable from time to time. In short, I want my students to do more than just hear about how the writing that they complete in school can improve the conditions of their lives—a statement that is true enough but too often lost on freshmen. Instead, I want them to initiate and then pursue for themselves their own personal transformations. In order for this to happen, I have to know my students as people, and I have to listen much more than I talk. This realization eluded me until I moved from a large school to a small one, and subsequently reconsidered my perceptions of students and my role as a writing teacher.

Of course, critics argue that it is not the job of English teachers to wade into the often turbulent waters of our students' personal lives. They will point out that most of us are not trained counselors, but that we are in fact accountable to other teachers, employers, taxpayers, trustees, and so on. Likewise, I know firsthand that some students resist invitations to probe publicly their personal lives in search of answers to the questions that genuinely confound them. Yet our best teachers are able to strike a balance. That is, they balance the expectations of outside agencies with their students' individual needs, whatever those needs might be. As a writing teacher and program administrator, my role is not to obsess about protecting either myself or my program as I did at ISU, but instead to facilitate my students' growth by helping them engage in those discursive explorations which are personally relevant to them. That's when their learning really begins.

I sensed these things when I was teaching at Illinois State, but I never understood the need for balance. Back then, my duty to the freshman composition course, the writing program, and the academy far outweighed my students' individual needs. At Findlay, I initially wrestled with what appeared to be the exact opposite set of circumstances before finally reconciling the two extremes for my students' benefit and my own.

If I had to pinpoint a moment when I began to swim in the complex currents of students' individual needs, institutional customs and practices, programmatic requirements, *and* modern theories of composition, it would have to be the day when I wrote a memo of my own about Helen W. and mailed it to the chair of Findlay's Academic Standards Committee. Among other things, I indicated that Helen was an intelligent young woman with "above average" writing ability, and I expressed my sincere desire to see her succeed in school and life beyond. I also explained that I would welcome her back into my class the following term provided that her medication had stabilized and she could attend a morning class regularly. I also agreed with the committee's decision to allow her to withdrawal from my course late instead of receiving the F—something I likely would not have done in the past. As I dropped the memo through the slot marked "Inter-Office Mail" in the basement of Old Main on the campus of The University of Findlay, I could not help but feel changed. I had discarded my old armor and replaced it with much lighter knee and elbow pads and a sturdy helmet. The fit, for me, remains dramatically more comfortable.

16

Plagiarism Might Go Away if We Don't Talk about It[1]

Jon Olson

Plagiarism, I thought as I read the paper. I'd had that thought before while reading students' papers as a composition teacher, but this time the butterflies in my stomach were on high alert. They brought dread, not just disappointment, because the stakes seemed higher in this particular composition scenario—a Master's thesis. This time, I wasn't the teacher leading twenty or thirty students in a conventional classroom; instead, I was the outside member of a thesis committee. Ours was a composition classroom broadly defined. I knew anything I might say as the perceived writing expert at the thesis defense would affect, one way or the other, the teaching and learning of writing for the graduate student and two other faculty members in the room.

All I could think was, "I can't sign this thesis. It's plagiarized." Or was it? I saw patches of writing in three distinct voices, styles, abilities. Should I take the time to investigate? I was reading the thesis near the end of Spring Break, and the defense was Monday. I felt sure if I said the word *plagiarism* in the meeting, even if merely invoking it with a "Could readers suspect?" question, I would turn the defense into a courtroom rather than a classroom.

The writer was an international student in a health science at a U.S. land-grant university.[2] I worried that I would be the only one on the committee who would point to evidence of plagiarism. The others on the committee had been in close contact with the writer during her writing process; I was the last one to read the thesis, having received it just prior to Spring Break. Now I didn't have much time. What would I do? I didn't see how I could avoid trouble. I couldn't in good conscience ignore the matter; however, mention of *plagiarism* would change me from a teacher to a judge, would change the student from a writer to a cheater, and would change the other committee members from mentors to members of a jury—or so I feared.

1. I thank Neal Lerner and Cheryl Glenn for their helpful responses to drafts of this essay.
2. Certain details have been changed to disguise identities.

For many reasons, I didn't want to turn that defense from a scholarly discussion of an interesting research project to an inquisition of moral wrongdoing. I cared about the committee chair, who was directing her first thesis in front of another committee member who was a powerful senior member of her department. I cared about the student, who was struggling with English to write some of the most engaging cross-cultural qualitative research I had read about perceptions of death and dying among hospice nurses. I cared about gender and power equity, for I was the only male on the committee. And as a compositionist, I cared more about teaching writing than policing it.

Solution? I didn't mention plagiarism once, and the problem went away.

After the defense, the chair was smiling as she collected willing signatures from each member of the committee on a document that said the student would pass if she fulfilled certain conditions of revision. The writer was eager to keep on writing. The senior member of the committee spoke for us all: "Boy, I really learned something about writing today." The writer did, in fact, complete her degree and went on to doctoral work. The last time I spoke with her, she said the defense taught her to see her writing as a unified whole rather than as a progression from one paragraph to another.

I can't take credit for that happy outcome. Credit goes to Rebecca Moore Howard (2000), author of "Sexuality, Textuality: The Cultural Work of Plagiarism." That article—a highly theorized feminist critique of academic culture—helped me reconsider my habits of mind and discover a more effective pedagogy. It gave me a view of student writing in which a problem vanished and an opportunity appeared.

What happened was that I experienced a fluke moment of good timing as I was stewing about the difficult situation I'd soon be facing in the thesis defense. My new issue of *College English* had just arrived, and I was drawn to Howard's piece because it was about plagiarism. The article hooked me as it opened by citing a sequence of surveys and articles in *The Council Chronicle* of the National Council of Teachers of English from November 1993 through September 1994 on how English teachers define plagiarism. They can't agree (p. 473). I could understand why they couldn't reach consensus, and what Howard went on to say rang true. She gave me a new way of thinking about plagiarism.

I admired Howard's intellectual finesse in arguing that "discourse on plagiarism regulates not only textuality but sexuality" (p. 474); it surely felt true that if I were to say in that committee, "I can't sign this thesis because I think it's plagiarized," that statement would be a sexually coded act. I'm still challenged to understand fully Howard's point: "gender, weakness, collaboration, disease, adultery, rape, heterosexuality, and property: This whole set of metaphors and associations lies behind every utterance of the word *plagiarism,* rendering fruitless our pedagogical efforts to teach useful textual strategies and to adjudicate this plagiarism thing" (p. 487). However, her analysis led to advice that saved the day for me: don't use the word *plagiarism;* instead, use other words such as *fraud* and *insufficient citation,* and shift attention to issues of pedagogy rather than issues of morality (p. 488).

Even if I had thought Howard's sexual–textual argument was nonsense (I don't think that, though some of my students do), her pedagogical advice at the end of the article would surely have served me well. However, her argument helped me notice potential dynamics of sex and gender on the committee, made me aware of the sexual and textual force I might wield if I carried the "plagiarism thing" into that setting. This awareness of possibilities helped me stop thinking, As a defender of academic virtue, I cannot sign this thesis in good conscience. Instead, Howard's argument got me to wondering, How can I be a composition teacher in this setting?

After reading Howard's piece, I resolved to listen to the writer and committee members to see what I could learn about their views of textual production, not bring up the word plagiarism at all, keep the focus on textual strategies such as coherence, voice, and unity of development, and be prepared simply to describe those features of the manuscript.

In the meeting, I soon had an opportunity to ask about the three voices I heard in the text. The voices seemed to be from (1) the non-native-speaker prose the writer used on email when she didn't have time to revise; (2) a near-native-fluency prose the writer achieved after she had worked on a section for a long time, perhaps with the guidance of her committee chair; and (3) edited academic published prose where published authors are invoked but where quotation marks are not used. I had decided not even to look for proof of plagiarism, choosing instead to talk about "patchwriting" (a word Howard uses to describe the kind of writing I thought I saw) in terms of unity, coherence, and cohesion. When the moment came, I kept attention on the text, not on the integrity of the author. I simply described my reading of the text, offering a list of page numbers where I heard each of the distinct voices in the manuscript. I asked how the writer and the committee wanted the text to sound.

One committee member wanted to keep the writer's unique international voice; another member wanted to make corrections so the thesis would be in "proper English." We discussed examples of the three voices, which included distinct styles of expression as well as patterns of development. We considered the relative merits of unity and coherence. The writer and committee ended up united in a desire to unify the text. The writer left that meeting grateful to her committee for the guidance she'd received, and she left with a plan that would make her thesis stronger. She would attend a series of writing workshops for graduate students who write in English as a second language, she would enroll in a course for international students writing theses and dissertations, and she would discuss her work with a peer consultant at the Graduate Writing Center.

We had focused on improving writing, not virtue. Consequently, we all learned something about writing from that difficult situation, thanks to a highly theoretical cultural critique that translated easily into practice. Although I did not receive a copy of the completed thesis before it was turned in (I did, after all, sign off on the thesis at the defense) and I didn't take the time to look up the thesis in the library, what I heard from the committee chair, from a Graduate Writing Center peer consultant, and from the writer herself, makes me think the revision efforts produced a unified document with sufficient citation. Best of all, the writer realized she had gained proficiency in her writing, once she noticed how different the parts she'd written at the beginning of her research were from the parts she'd written at the end. It didn't make her writing process any easier when she discovered how academic writers mold paragraphs and chapters into a unified whole, when she realized that the writing process doesn't end when the final paragraph has been extruded. She did, however, seem to enter the next level of her academic research with more confidence as a writer and scholar. And I think about that difficult teaching situation with relief.

The plagiarism went away because we didn't talk about it.

Works Cited

Howard, Rebecca Moore. "Sexuality, Textuality: The Cultural Work of Plagiarism." *College English* 62.4 (March 2000): 473–91.

17

Room for "Us" to Play

The Teacher as Midwife

Matthew Parfitt

It felt like we were at war with each other, this class and I, and I could not explain how we had reached this point or see how to move past it. On one particular wet Tuesday in March, the undercurrent of discontent became unmistakable. One of the brightest and most articulate students in the class—I'll call him "Kevin"—had his head on his forearms and his eyes closed. He was, I supposed, not actually sleeping, but resting his eyes or lightly napping. Either way, I knew it to be a gesture of defiance and disaffection, intended to speak for the entire group of fourteen, and I felt precisely as irritated and humiliated as he could have wished. From this moment forward, unless something changed drastically, discussion would be an uphill battle and writing a mere perfunctory chore.

I had feared such a stand-off or impasse for some weeks and thought I had taken steps to avoid it, but I'd underestimated the depth of the problem. Right now, I was feeling vaguely nauseated: I'd experienced this kind of thing years before, when first tossed into a classroom as a grad student, and heard of it happening to others, and knew how difficult it could be to dig out of this kind of a pit. But here I was up for tenure, and expecting senior faculty to visit my classroom at any moment, unannounced. As a class, we were seven months into our nine-month journey, and I was pushing against these students, pushing them uphill. Kevin's nap spoke about as loudly as napping can: they were having none of it. The more they resisted, the harder I pushed—and the more I tried to be indirect or good-humored about it, the more passive–aggressive I was seeming. We were all beginning to sense that the class was spinning into some sort of irreversible death spiral.

This Kevin, I thought to myself, was part of the problem. Tall, neat, and self-assured, he was a student leader type, and in some way the catalyst of the stand-off, though it would be unfair to say he was responsible for it. Back in

September, he had been eager to make a good impression, and he did: his writing was elegant and error-free, and he could construct an argument that would hold the reader's interest, even if seeming a little far-fetched. But soon, as we began to work more closely with layered, complex texts, his polemics began to seem reductive and facile. In conference, he told me that he had been captain of his high school debating team (no surprise there) and had discovered that he could transport his debating skills into his writing: by relying on a few strong and adaptable rhetorical strategies, he could consistently produce essays that earned him praise and good grades. In effect, he proudly specialized in the far-fetched: "You have to find an issue and then take a really strong stand," he explained, "and no matter how unlikely or extreme your position is, you need to defend it as ingeniously as you can and you need to knock down the arguments that might be made against it." This exactly described his approach to my assignments—even those that called for something quite different, something more probing or exploratory or autobiographical.

I wanted him to try out new kinds of argument, less formulaic and artificial, more open to genuine inquiry and sincere engagement with questions and problems. So I posed a challenge to him by describing a more exploratory kind of essay, exemplified by those we'd been reading this semester [Richard Rodriguez's (2002) "The Achievement of Desire," Walker Percy's (2002) "The Loss of the Creature," Clifford Geertz's (2002) "Deep Play: Notes on the Balinese Cockfight"]. Kevin understood; he seemed excited, even flattered, that I was suggesting he was ready to move past the more elementary models of our writer's handbook and to think of his writing as a vehicle for real inquiry, an opportunity to engage in mature and sophisticated thinking. I looked forward to his next essay.

But the essay proved disappointing: It did show a willingness to experiment, but there was no development, no sense of purpose or engagement. It was really just a series of thoughts, hypotheses, and questions that amounted to very little. Perhaps he had supposed that a less rigidly structured, less disputatious essay required less discipline and carefulness. I tried in my comments to point out both the essay's strengths and its weaknesses, but knew it deserved a grade no better than C+ (the average grade at our college being a C). Kevin told me he felt penalized for taking my advice: He should have received a better grade because, after all, he'd taken the risks I wanted him to take. I encouraged him to try again, but next time Kevin simply returned to his tried-and-true methods. By February, our dialogue was beginning to feel unproductive: a battle rather than a conversation.

And somehow Kevin's resentment had infected the entire class. How this happened, I am still not quite sure. My college's tough grading standards and its required curriculum mean that instructors always have to earn the students' goodwill, but our team structure (students and faculty are grouped into teams of about 120) typically produces a trust and closeness that make it possible to do so before second semester. In this case, however, Kevin's antagonism had become more than a mood or temper; it represented an intellectual style that justified its own opposition to the objectives of my course, a style that polarized ideas into winners and losers and relegated ambiguity and uncertainty to the losing side. And part of the problem (I realized later) was that my own style in the classroom unwittingly participated in, and reinforced, this antagonistic, oppositional style: in trying to challenge students to look beyond simplistic or superficial interpretations of texts and problems, my style of discussion leading had become, from their point of view, similarly confrontational and antagonizing. Debate might have been a valuable tool a month or two earlier, but debate thrives in an atmosphere of friendly competition, and the atmosphere of this classroom had become competitive in a distinctly unfriendly way. Ideally, however, what we needed was not debate but conversation, genuinely open and exploratory conversation, yet I could not see how to lead such a conversation without it becoming idle or pointless. Wasn't it necessary, after all, to push students toward stronger, closer readings of the text and more adequate responses to it? How to fulfill these two goals: to guide discussion in a way that showed greater respect for the students' ideas—even their most wayward ideas—and yet avoid suggesting that "all opinions are equally valid"?

Looking back, I'm not sure there was much I could have done with that class at that moment: being in the middle of a difficult, contested tenure process in which exemplary teaching counted even more than publications, I had to plan classes carefully so that each separate class somehow reflected my goals for the course and produced at least the appearance of success. I couldn't realistically take the risks that a different kind of teaching would require. But while our texts and our assignments exemplified a spirit of experimentation, free inquiry, and even playfulness that I professed to admire and value, my strenuous efforts were only making the class more of a burden—to myself and to the students: I was bringing my own anxiety about tenure into each of our classes, and I had become inflexible, willful, joyless. I'm not sure whether students were conscious of the discrepancy, but I'm sure that my single-minded determination must have become more tiresome, certainly more inescapable, than Kevin's heavy-handed polemics had ever been for me.

As I reflected on this class, I realized soon enough that it only exposed a more general problem in my teaching, a contradiction between the way I prepared for discussion and what I really hoped would transpire. When lively discussions did take place in my classes, they seemed to do so almost despite my efforts: my practice, typically, was to solicit students' answers to the kind of carefully prepared question that only a teacher would ask, ones that quizzed students on their comprehension, or asked them to reflect on a problem or issue that was really *my* problem or issue. At times, students must have felt required to guess what I was thinking. All "discussion" passed through me, the teacher, and students often hardly interacted with one another at all. Most students must have found this pretty pointless, but there were always four or five eager students who gamely keep this kind of discussion going. Even if no lively conversation erupted, the discussion would hobble along through fifty minutes of class time and everyone went away feeling like a discussion had taken place whether it involved them or not. Kevin, I began to think, had the intelligence to see through this kind of game and too much integrity to play it.

Initially, I was inclined to consider the whole problem in terms of some failure of my own as a teacher, and even as a human being. In *The Courage to Teach,* Parker Palmer (1998) argues persuasively that "good teaching cannot be reduced to technique; good teaching comes from the identity and integrity of the teacher" (p. 10). But however true this may be as a general rule, self-examination and soul-searching proved not to be especially helpful to me as I thought about this particular class. The reason, I think, is that the more I thought of something in *myself* as responsible for the problem, the more I was separating myself from the class and thereby reinstating the problem. Instead, I needed to shift my perspective, and begin to look at the situation as one that *involved* me, but did not rest with me.

In the months that followed, I reflected on the importance of sustaining a different kind of "game" in my course. Genuine conversation is a kind of play. I was reminded of Hans-Georg Gadamer's (1975–1989) discussion of the significance of "play" in *Truth and Method.* In order for a game to emerge, the players must lose themselves in the play, and allow the requirements of the game to take over and absorb their attention and their will; thus, play exists as something separate from—over and above—the subjectivity of individual players: "Play has its own essence, independent of the consciousness of those who play" (p. 102). Gadamer invokes the concept of play for his own philosophical purpose—to argue that works of art have a "mode of being" that cannot be described in terms of a subject confronting an object—but it seemed to me a useful concept for pedagogy too. In a discussion class, something must emerge that transcends individual subjectivities, that has its own essence, that must be nurtured and sustained but cannot be controlled or even directed. The give-and-take of class discussion must remain unpredictable. There are rules and objectives, but these rules do not restrict the play, they make it possible. In Kevin's class, as in others, I had been too eager to remain in control, and this eagerness subtly eroded the spontaneity of classroom discussion, an erosion that students probably sensed, even if unconsciously.

But how to promote genuine conversation and still ensure that it would be useful and productive? How to cede control of the discussion without ceding control of the course objectives? I still see no easy answer, but I began to find that being a little more gentle, a little less talkative and a lot less anxious, helps considerably. The following year, I stopped preparing questions for discussion and instead began to focus on employing simple "structures" that would ensure that every student came to class with something to say, something thoughtful and informed. This might be a simple homework assignment involving a dialectical notebook exercise (see Berthoff, 1988, p. 26ff.) or a low-stakes in-class "quiz" that really functioned as an opportunity for reflection. The point was to use the students' responses to the text as the starting point for discussion, and then simply nurture the conversation as it unfolded. I would intervene chiefly to clarify or to complicate, and when for some reason the conversation came to a halt, my task would be somehow to get the play going again. I had always thought of my approach to discussion as vaguely "Socratic," but I had mostly been using question-and-answer as a way of guiding students to some kind of "right answer," an answer already known to me, the teacher. True Socratic method, I began to see, is maieutic: that is, the teacher acts as an intellectual midwife; he or she assists the "mother" (the student) in bringing to birth ideas that the midwife has not foreseen, any more than the mother. But the new ideas truly *belong* to the mother, not the midwife. This is the only way that ideas in the true sense can ever be born and they are obviously much greater and more powerful than "right answers."

But this could only be done if I as the teacher remained attentive to the "us" that brings the game to life and sustains it. I had often noticed that class sections develop a kind of corporate personality that was somehow more than, or different from, the sum of the individuals within it, and how individuals somehow fitted themselves to this corporate personality. Kevin's class was a negative case in point, but I could think of positive cases too. I had tended to see this corporate personality as a product of "them," the students, rather than of me-and-them together. To see the class as an "us" means to relinquish the sense of a me and a them, while not abdicating my responsibilities as the teacher, the mature adult presence, the final arbiter of the course's objectives, and, of course, the grader. These roles, instead, become elements in an "us," a unique reality that evolves out of our encounters with one another inside and outside the classroom. When Paulo Freire (1970) writes in *Pedagogy of the Oppressed* of the "new term" that emerges in problem-posing education, "teacher–student with students–teachers," he does not mean, I think, that the teacher no longer has a defined role in a student-centered classroom—or if he does, then his pedagogy has to be revised to meet the realities of American undergraduate education. I would prefer to think that he means that a corporate entity emerges that transcends all the individual persons within it, including the teacher, and that the teacher must commit him or herself to this entity, nurture it, attend to it, believe in it.

In *Reason to Believe: Romanticism, Pragmatism and the Teaching of Writing,* Hephzibah Roskelly and Kate Ronald (1998) expound a "romantic/pragmatic" pedagogy, an approach to teaching that seeks to move dialectically between, on the one hand, the romanticism of ideals and theories and, on the other, the pragmatics of the classroom. Drawing on the American tradition of romantic pragmatism, particularly on Emerson, Thoreau, William James, and Dewey, they present this pedagogy as a way out of the impasse to which postmodern antifoundationalism has brought us. Their approach refuses to withdraw into theory as an intellectual game with no real bearing on practice—but it also refuses to abandon theory in the cynical pursuit of merely expedient objectives. The result is what they unblushingly describe as a "pedagogy of love": one that is grounded in respect for students and belief in the value of education, "an exploration of love and hope as principled methods for teaching literacy" (Roskelly and Ronald, 1998, p. 162).

Returning to Gadamer (1975–1989) and the hermeneutic tradition, I think of this romantic/pragmatic dialectic as a kind of hermeneutic circle: It is a circle in that it moves restlessly back and forth between the generalized principles of theory and the specific facts of a particular classroom; it is hermeneutic in that it represents an endless task of reinterpreting the one in terms of the other. It means that the task of the teacher is never quite "given," never entirely clear; he or she must constantly improvise and revise. Further, it means that, if the responsibility for articulating and safeguarding the goals of the course rests principally with me as the teacher, I will be circling dialectically between "my" ideals and the students' realities, continually reinterpreting the one in terms of the other. In effect, this circling means that the two poles—the ideal and the real, the teacher (me) and the students (them)—become subsumed in the movement which I have been calling "us." My experience with Kevin taught me how vital and real this "us" is.

Works Cited

Berthoff, Ann E., with James Stephens. 1988. *Forming/Thinking/Writing*. 2nd ed. Portsmouth, NH: Heinemann/Boynton-Cook.

Freire, Paulo. 1970. *Pedagogy of the Oppressed*. Trans. Myra Bergman Ramos. New York: Seabury P.

Gadamer, Hans-Georg. 1975–1989. *Truth and Method*. 2nd revised edition. Trans. Joel Weinsheimer and Donald G. Marshall. New York: Crossroad.

Geertz, Clifford. 2002. "Deep Play: Notes on the Balinese Cockfight." In *Ways of Reading: An Anthology for Writers*. 6th edition, edited by David Bartholomae and Anthony Petrosky, 305–339. Boston: Bedford–St. Martins.

Palmer, Parker J. 1998. *The Courage to Teach: Exploring the Inner Landscape of a Teacher's Life*. San Francisco: Jossey-Bass.

Percy, Walker. 2002. "The Loss of Creature." In *Ways of Reading: An Anthology for Writers*. 6th edition, edited by David Bartholomae and Anthony Petrosky (Eds.), 588–601. Boston: Bedford–St. Martins.

Roskelly, Hephzibah and Kate Ronald. 1998. *Reason to Believe: Romanticism, Pragmatism and the Teaching of Writing*. New York: SUNY Press.

Rodriguez, Richard. 2002. "The Achievement of Desire." In *Ways of Reading: An Anthology for Writers*. 6th edition, edited by David Bartholomae and Anthony Petrosky, 652–670. Boston: Bedford–St. Martins.

Afterword

Difficulty for Whom?: Teachers' Discourse About Difficult Students

Hugh English

Two years ago, in my second semester at Queens College, I taught a senior writing-intensive seminar for English majors in which we read Gertrude Stein and Willa Cather in the contexts of historically constructed and contested categories of sex/gender and sexuality. While reading varied literary forms, we considered these writers' textual and historical resistances to, evasions of, and engagements with identity categories such as "woman" and "lesbian." On the day that I was being observed by my department Chair, one student, in his presentation, began a discussion of "butch/femme" as a way of understanding the characters and the central relationship represented in Stein's (1998) *The Autobiography of Alice B. Toklas.* As I listened, I was impressed with his use of these gender terms, specific enough to lesbian and other queer cultures that I had not anticipated their introduction into our conversation unless I introduced them. (Obviously, from my surprise, you will gather that no students in the class had identified themselves as lesbian, gay, or queer; nor were any of the students legible as such to me.)

Suddenly, another student exploded in anger at the use of these terms, based apparently on his perception of the first student as "not-gay" and on his defensive revelation that his mother is a lesbian. By claiming an inside position of authentic knowledge, one student attacked another as supposedly homophobic. In contrast, I had been pleasantly surprised by what I took to be a sophisticated and intelligent effort to explore the valences of these gender terms as a way of reading Stein's lesbian codes in her autobiographical project. It was an uncomfortable moment, perhaps especially for me in my second semester with my Chair observing me, but certainly for other students too. In my salvage attempt, I introduced explicitly a discussion of the contexts of naming, offering a brief history of the contest within women's history over "butch/femme" experiences, and making a case for understanding these gender terms both as related to heterosexual gender terms and as a queer revision of them.

My Chair's observation generously put it this way: "This was a very heated moment, but it was beautifully mediated by Professor English." In passing, let me note, that I'm aware that it could have gone differently. More to the point, as I have come to realize, this "heated moment" represents also the sort of teaching moment that I'm aiming for—a moment in which words and naming and

119

their contexts take center stage in ways that matter to those participating in the conversation. It has taken me longer, however, to begin to understand the value of the angry explosion. By breaking the decorum of the classroom, my "difficult" student (and, yes, he was consistently that) shifted the energy of the seminar conversation, stimulating an extra level of attention and involvement from each student, myself, and my supervising Chair.

At issue here are excess and the limits of classroom discourse—what exceeds allowable meanings in teacher and student language, what can be said and what can't be said, how much feeling or affect can be expressed, what versions of self are appropriately performed by me and by my students. In addition to stimulating what turned into an interesting conversation about the terms "butch/femme" and their cultural and historical locations, the "difficult" student—no matter how much he annoyed or even offended me and other students—gave us the gift of awareness of what might otherwise remain invisible: he marked the edges of allowable discourse and made difficulty for my previously unperturbed (albeit relatively) persona as a teacher. By challenging the allowable discourse of my classroom, he taught me about my fear of losing rhetorical and epistemological and emotional control, even when I think I've surrendered some of my authority (that fantasy) in the interests of students' engagement in making meaning. The difficult student and moment bring me back to the reality of the edges in my classroom. In this case, by posing both pedagogical and social difficulties, a student's excess opened a space where I could reinvestigate my own authority.

Reconsidered in this way, I see my own fear of losing professional and rhetorical control, especially in front of my Chair. (Given that it was still my first year at Queens, I couldn't know yet how her thoughtfulness about teaching and her experience as a teacher would lead her to understand this "heated moment.") One student's explosion, transgressing the etiquette of academic discourse, raises questions for me about what I allow myself and my students to say and to perform in the classroom. What sort of discursive world am I setting up for my students' assimilation? What is the place of "feeling" in this discursive world? How do our emotional responses shape our intellectual work? Why didn't I move the class toward a discussion of the "feelings" raised in this "heated moment"? (Barry Manilow, in the background. Yecch! What's this "Yecch" about?) Would I have been seen as having "beautifully mediated" this "very heated moment" if I had more explicitly engaged all of our feelings?

One thing I do know is that I didn't do so because I don't want to fathom fully some of my students' homophobia and heterosexism, although I clearly want to engage their minds in thinking about sex/gender, sexuality, and institutional and ideological heterosexuality. Yet, it strikes me that, in an explicit move to a discussion of feeling, I would be putting my students' responses to "homosexuality," their possible homophobia, within sight, allowing homophobia possibly, heterosexism almost certainly, to become visible and articulate, in ways that could be very, very uncomfortable for me as a queer person. Was I trying to be a professional in the sense of separating my "personal" stake from my pedagogical stake? Yes, of course. And, that's necessary. But where and when do I define the edges of my own difficult, untenured, queer location in the classroom and in the academy?

This anecdote—like so many others that teachers share with one another *about* their students—teaches about what exceeds rhetorically and epistemologically the limits of classroom discourse and about how certain behaviors and certain performances of self are marked as acceptable and others as unacceptable. This anecdote, in other words, is also *about* a teacher and his particular version of the classroom, as much as it is about students. In retrospect, I think that I might have gone further into the feelings being expressed, and I may have done so if I were not so obviously, in that classroom moment, also literally and immediately within an institutional relationship as an untenured professor being observed by my Chair. As I think about these issues, I remember my pain, in my first couple of years as a teaching assistant at Rutgers University, when students dismissed Adrienne Rich's (1999) complex and personal essay about women and writing, "When We Dead Awaken: Writing as Re-Vision," because the editors, necessarily in discussing Rich's work, identify her as a lesbian in their introductory note. I remember, in some semesters, choosing *not* to teach Rich's essay because I didn't want to feel pain in the face of my students' homophobic responses. And, I didn't want to expose my own fear and "difficulty," nor endure the painful contradiction of professional objectivity in the face of responses that threatened my own subjectivity.

To what extent, then, do I let my fear of emotional difficulty edit my curricula? Obviously, not always, as the curricular context of my opening anecdote should make clear. Yet, there are other times. For example, last semester in my Composition class, I taught Cindy Sherman's (2000) photography, together with a group of faculty teaching courses linked in a learning community. In planning for our group symposium on Sherman's provocative self-representations, it was "obvious" to us that we didn't want to include her edgy photographs of prosthetic genitalia: why? To what extent were we invested in maintaining our own control and in avoiding prospective or potential difficult moments in our classrooms and in our institution? Is it possible to be in control of the difficult moments that may open for our use?

This semester, my Composition class is linked with an American Studies class in which students will look at the *Declaration of Independence*. While preparing, I enthusiastically played with the idea of teaching rhetorical citations of that text, including the Seneca Falls (1996) *Declaration of Sentiments* and Patti Smith's recent and revolutionary version of the *Declaration of Independence* on a live recording of her song, "Rock'n Roll Nigger" (1998), and in a song, "New Party," on her new cd, *Gung Ho* (2000). Then, as I thought about it, I realized that I was not at all certain that I wanted to introduce the word "nigger" into my classroom, at least not without carefully raising a much larger historical context of racial and racist naming and the citation of those names by African-Americans and by Patti Smith. Certainly, such a conversation about words and their contexts and about words and power would be entirely appropriate to my course goals. However, I decided not to teach Smith's text, based partly on the realization that I would be unable to do a lot of other things because of the time it would take to offer sufficient context for her use of the word. But I know that I'm also thinking as I make this decision: Do I really want to experience this discomfort in the classroom? Do I really want to risk being misunderstood as a supposedly "white" person using the "n" word? Why not take the easier route?

Moreover—and this is also important—how can I teach Smith without playing her louder than my faculty neighbors will tolerate? Last year, my use of Lauryn Hill's (1998) *The Miseducation of Lauryn Hill* led to a request to turn the music down, despite the fact that we had endured the loud drone of this particular professor's monological lectures all semester. I felt like a teenager in my parent's house. The choice of Smith's text, heard at what I take to be an appropriate volume, would quite literally go beyond the limits of acceptable discourse in the material, architectural space of my classroom.

In any event, my interest, here, is in the acts of editing, even censorship, that we perform in order to homogenize the classroom in our "teacherly" images, in order to avoid crossing those lines that threaten one's sense of being a professional teacher, and certainly also in order to avoid transgressing boundaries that would get us in trouble within the institution, especially if we are untenured faculty. Is this not how institutions reproduce themselves? Avoiding my own "difficulty" is a necessary and sane response to difficult negotiations, to my negotiations of difficulty, but examining such avoidance is also useful for its revelation of what exceeds the discursive limits of my classroom.

When Composition teachers gather around our proverbial water coolers, we share stories of our experiences with students. Sometimes those stories tell of encouraging successes, sometimes of frustrations, and sometimes of the particular challenges of "difficult situations," or even "difficult students." We share stories in our search for new understandings and responses, but our teacher discourse rarely moves beyond the assumed limits of our classroom goals and the worlds that those goals take for granted.

"Difficult situations" offer moments of potential disruption of the world that I assume as a classroom teacher. The implicit contract between teacher and student breaks down with the student who won't wait to speak or the student who explicitly challenges the goals of the course or the student who explodes in anger or in tears. Rather than tell a story with a familiar narrative of a creative teacher's inventive response to "difficulty" (notice the comforting movement from crisis to resolution), I have been trying to tell about coming to see how "difficult situations" can productively threaten the classroom as a world made in my image. Certainly I necessarily and perhaps inevitably assert my authority and the authority of the academic institution behind me when faced with "difficulty" or resistance, but even as I do so I try *not* to miss seeing the productive challenge to a world centered around my teacherly persona. I try to see how conflict and "difficulty" and the power to apply those labels foreground how a classroom is homogenized from a teacher's vantage point [to paraphrase Mary Louise Pratt (1999) in "Arts of the Contact Zone"].

We necessarily teach within power relations and institutional cultures that precede and follow us, and we can certainly never be entirely outside of those relations and cultures. However, as we play our teacherly roles, we might also notice them as roles; we might also see the limits of the world centered around our rules for oral and literate exchanges, and, in so doing, we can at least change the ways that we talk about students and *their* difficulties (or the difficulties they pose for us) as we gather around the proverbial water cooler or wherever we find ourselves in teacher discourse. The lesson of letting go of (or, perhaps better, of holding more lightly to) the rules, values, and goals of my discursive world remains ahead. I have been teaching in colleges for fifteen years. With more and more experience, I find myself more and more skilled at these delicate negotiations. I also find myself less and less certain of the boundaries of allowable discourse and the acceptable performances of self in my classrooms. Perhaps, in this case, experience teaches me to know less and to feel okay about that.

Works Cited

Bartholomae, David and Anthony Petrosky. 1999. *Ways of Reading: An Anthology for Writers.* 5th ed. New York: Bedford St. Martin's.

Bizzell, Patricia and Bruce Herzberg. 1996. *Negotiating Difference: Cultural Case Studies for Composition.* New York: Bedford St. Martin's.

Hill, Lauryn. 1998. *The Miseducation of Lauryn Hill.* Ruffhouse.

Jefferson, Thomas. 1996. "Draft of the Declaration of Independence." In *Negotiating Difference: Cultural Case Studies for Composition,* edited by Patricia Bizzell and Bruce Herzberg, 174–79. New York: Bedford St. Martin's.

Pratt, Mary Louise. 1999. "Arts of the Contact Zone." In *Ways of Reading: An Anthology for Writers,* 5th ed., edited by David Bartholomae and Anthony Petrosky, 581–600. New York: Bedford St. Martin's.

Rich, Adrienne. 1999. "When We Dead Awaken: Writing as Re-Vision." In *Ways of Reading: An Anthology for Writers,* 5th ed., edited by David Bartholomae and Anthony Petrosky, 601–619. New York: Bedford St. Martin's.

Seneca Falls Women's Rights Convention. 1996. "Declaration of Sentiments and Resolutions." In *Negotiating Difference: Cultural Case Studies for Composition,* edited by Patricia Bizzell and Bruce Herzberg, 387–90. New York: Bedford St. Martin's.

Sherman, Cindy. 2000. *Retrospective.* 2nd ed. New York: Thames and Hudson.

Smith, Patti. 2000. "New Party." *Gung Ho.* Arista.

———. 1999. "Rock 'n Roll Nigger (Recorded Live in Chicago, 11/22/98)." *New Party* (Limited Edition). Arista.

Stein, Gertrude. 1998. *The Autobiography of Alice B. Toklas.* In *Gertrude Stein: Early Writings 1903–1932,* edited by Catharine R. Stimpson and Harriet Chessman, 653–913. New York: Library of America.

Contributors

Linda Adler-Kassner continues to work with students-called-basic-writers in her position at Eastern Michigan University, where she also works with graduate students teaching first year composition in her capacity as a writing program administrator. Her most recent book, coauthored with Susanmarie Harrington, is *Basic Writing as a Political Act: Public Conversations about Writing and Literacies* (Hampton Press).

Victoria Arthur is currently a Ph.D. student and T.A. at Washington State University, where her academic interests include both the pedagogy of composition and nineteenth-century British Literature. She brings experience teaching composition at Western Washington University (while getting her Master's in English Studies) and at Skagit Valley and Whatcom Community colleges, where some of the most useful pedagogical lessons she learned were provided by her so-called "basic" students in English 95 and 100.

Ann Dean is Assistant Professor of English and Director of College Writing at the University of Southern Maine. Her book *Teaching Literature: A Companion,* coedited with Tanya Agathocleous, is forthcoming from Palgrave. Her research interests include composition studies and eighteenth-century print culture.

Paul W. DePasquale is of Mohawk and European backgrounds and a member of the Six Nations of the Grand River Reserve in Ontario, Canada. He is an Assistant Professor of English at the University of Winnipeg, Manitoba, where he publishes in the areas of Aboriginal Studies and Early Modern Culture, with an emphasis on early colonialism and representations of Aboriginal peoples. A former Fulbright scholar, Paul is the editor of the forthcoming special issue, "Natives and Settlers Then and Now: Past and Present Perspectives on Aboriginal Issues in Canada, United States, and New Zealand," *Canadian Review of Comparative Literature,* and coeditor of *Telling Our Stories: Omushkego Voices from Hudson Bay* (Broadview Press, forthcoming). He also publishes fiction and poetry.

Suzanne Diamond is Assistant Professor of English at Youngstown State University. She received her Ph.D. from Rutgers University in 1996, where she began teaching in 1989. She has directed writing centers at Rutgers and at Marietta College, and is coeditor of *Literacies: Reading, Writing, Interpretation,* a composition textbook published by W.W. Norton.

Born in North Hykeham, Lincolnshire, **Stephen Dilks** (Ph.D. Rutgers) is a Literacy Specialist and Assistant Professor of modern and contemporary English/Irish Literature at UMKC. He is currently writing a book called *Inventing the Modern Writer* and has presented and published essays on Samuel Beckett, Edna O'Brien, James Joyce, Dennis Potter, Virginia Woolf, and the teaching of reading and writing. He is coauthor of *Cultural Conversations: The Presence of the Past* (Bedford St. Martins, 2001).

At Queens College in the City University of New York, **Hugh English** regularly teaches the first-year writing course, required and elective courses in the English major, and courses on Composition Theory/Literacy Studies and on Modern Literature in the MA Program. As Coordinator of College Writing Programs, he also works to develop and to coordinate college-wide efforts in Writing Across the Curriculum. His current research includes a book-length study of Gertrude Stein's imaginative invention of "America" in the face of European crisis and war in the 1930s and 1940s, and projects in several areas of contemporary Composition Studies, most notably on the ways that we understand the work of "administration" in Composition, on the discourses of class in Composition, and on how our students understand and articulate their reading practices.

Deborah Gussman is Assistant Professor of Literature at the Richard Stockton College of New Jersey, where she teaches courses in American literature and culture, rhetoric and composition, and women's studies. She recently published "Republican Rhetoric and Subversity: Women, Indians, and Citizenship in the 1820's," in *Professing Rhetoric* (ed. Frederick Antzcak; Lawrence Erlbaum Associates). Her current research focuses on rhetorics of social reform in writings by American Indians and women in the early nineteenth century.

Susanmarie Harrington is Director of Writing and Associate Professor of English at Indiana University Purdue University Indianapolis. Her work has appeared in the *Journal of Basic Writing, WPA,* and *Computers and Composition.* With Linda Adler-Kassner, she is the author of *Basic Writing as a Political Act* (Hampton Press).

Christine Jespersen is an Assistant Professor of English at Western State College, where she teaches literature and composition courses. Her areas of expertise are in nineteenth and twentieth century American literature. Currently, she is working on a book about adventure writing at the turn of the last century.

T. R. Johnson is an Assistant Professor of English and Director of the Writing Center at the University of New Orleans. His work mixes theoretical and historical discourse, and it has appeared in *The Journal of Advanced Composition* and *College Composition and Communication.*

Eric V. Martin is the Assistant Provost/Director of the Center for Quality at Governors State University (Illinois). He coordinates assessment, faculty development, and writing across the curriculum. Before accepting a position at Governors State, Martin was an assistant professor of English at The University of Findlay (Ohio), where he directed the English and WAC programs. He has taught introductory through graduate-level writing courses as well as courses on the teaching of writing.

Jon Olson directs The Pennsylvania State University's Center for Excellence in Writing that includes an Undergraduate Writing Center (coordinated in collaboration with the University Learning Centers), a Graduate Communication Enhancement Program (which has a Graduate Writing Center), and a Writing Across the Curriculum Program. His scholarly interests include composition, rhetoric, writing administration, and American slave narratives. He has authored articles for *The Writing Instructor, Writing Lab Newsletter,* and *Teaching with Writing;* and for the edited collections *The Place of Grammar in Writing Instruction, The Writing Center Resource Manual,* and *Writing Center Research.* He serves on the boards of the International Writing Centers Association, the

Mid-Atlantic Writing Centers Association, and the National Conference on Peer Tutoring in Writing.

Matthew Parfitt is Associate Professor in the Division of Humanities and Rhetoric at the College of General Studies, Boston University. With Regina Hansen and Stephen Dilks, he is the author of *Cultural Conversations: The Presence of the Past* (Bedford St. Martins, 2001). He has published articles and presented papers on composition, hermeneutics, and World War I literature. He may be reached at *parfitt@bu.edu.*

Priscilla Perkins directs the Composition Program and teaches American literature at Roosevelt University in Chicago and Schaumburg, Illinois. Her composition research focuses on connections between academic and religious hermeneutics, as well as on faculty development strategies. She is a coauthor of *Literacies: Reading, Writing, Interpretation* (W.W. Norton).

Brad Peters coordinates the writing across the curriculum program at Northern Illinois University and serves as Acting Director of the Writing Center. He teaches theory and history of rhetoric/composition, professional writing, and tutoring in writing. He has published on critical pedagogy, feminisms, and medieval rhetorics of the English mystics.

John Regan is Assistant Professor of Rhetoric at the College of General Studies at Boston University Studies. His publications include essays on the Ursuline convent riot and the literature of John P. Marquand. He has presented papers at numerous national and regional conferences including the MLA and SHARP. In 1999, he served as the Chair of the Executive Committee of the Modern Language Association's Discussion Group on Part-Time Faculty. His current book project is a study of antebellum convent captivity narratives.

Dawn Skorczewski is Director of Freshman Writing and Assistant Professor at Emerson College. She is preparing a book manuscript entitled *Teaching Writing One Moment at a Time,* an exploration of intersections between intersubjective psychoanalytic theory and the teaching of writing. She has published articles on composition in *College Composition and Communication* and *Stories Told in School,* and on representations of father–daughter incest in poetry in *Signs: A Journal of Women, Culture, and Society.*